Have a Nice
Day

JUSTIN WEBB

First published in 2008 by
Short Books
3A Exmouth House
Pine Street
London EC1R 0JH

This paperback edition published in 2009
10 9 8 7 6 5 4 3 2 1

978-1-906021-70-2
Printed in England by CPI Bookmarque, Croydon
Jacket design: Jon Gray

To my mother
and to Sarah, Martha, Sam and Clara

Contents

Introduction

*My anti-Americanism has become almost uncontrollable.
It has possessed me, like a disease. It rises up in my throat
like acid reflux, that fashionable American sickness. I now
loathe the United States and what it has done to Iraq and
the rest of the helpless world… I hate feeling this hatred. I
have to keep reminding myself that if Bush hadn't been (so
narrowly) elected, we wouldn't be here, and none of this
would have happened. There is another America. Long live
the other America, and may this one pass away soon.*

Margaret Drabble, 2003

*… To all other peoples and governments who are watching
today, from the grandest capitals to the small village where
my father was born: know that America is a friend of each
nation and every man, woman, and child who seeks a
future of peace and dignity, and that we are ready to lead
once more.*

Barack Obama, Inaugural Address, 2009

A SCOTTISH LABOUR MP told me a story that sums up this
moment in the history of America and the world. He'd been

9

texted by his son on the night of Barack Obama's election triumph. The teenage boy – who had never shown the tiniest scintilla of interest in dad's political career – sent two words: "WE WON!"

America is cool. Just as black is the new blonde in polite American society, so the stars and stripes are the new *tricolour*, or whatever yesterday's cool flag was. Will it last? The closure of Guantanamo Bay will help. So will Team Obama's rational approach to scientific facts, on global warming etc. The very sight of Obama hopping off Air Force One lifts the spirits of some. But there is more to America than Obama and his people, just as there was more to America than Bush and his folks. Obama's America is a starburst of human life but the starburst did not start with him. This book is a journey through a nation embracing change, but a journey as well through a nation enjoying continuity, a nation whose heart, in my view, has always been in the right place.

In fact, it's our foreign hearts that we should be concerned about: in particular our stony, European tickers.

When I was a boy growing up in the city of Bath, my mother – a Quaker and pacifist – used to take me on Saturdays to see her friends in the Abbey Churchyard. They were protesters, these friends. Genteel and sensibly shod, they hung around outside the grand doors of this central monument, handing out leaflets and engaging in banter with passing acquaintances. They were good people, thoughtful and peaceful. But as I grew older I began to notice something rather odd about their pet causes. Their heartfelt protests against nuclear weapons, for instance, concentrated on American warheads, not the Soviet missiles in those days pointed directly at us. When they campaigned against war, it was American-led war they abhorred. Against executions? In Texas of course…

These seemed to me to be more than attacks on the things America did. They were part of a general attitude towards America and the world, an ideology whose central tenet was that *the Yanks are to blame*. Without realizing it, without consciously willing it, Mum's friends were anti-Americans. And this was before even Ronald Reagan; long before George W Bush. Even then everything upsetting was American, everything worthy of condemnation and protest had an address ending in a zip code.

Nothing much has changed. On occasions European dislike of America comes close to racism. It is a deeply felt prejudice. Why else would English friends with impeccable anti-racist credentials ask of our children (who have grown up in the US) "how will you get rid of their accents?" They assume, without ever questioning why, that we would want to…

For many Europeans, hating America, (or in the case of peaceful Quakers, disliking it intensely) comes easily and always has done. But I want to suggest that it is a mistake and that this moment in history – this Obama moment – is as good a moment as any for a rethink. Like the junk food Americans so famously consume, contempt for America is cheap, unsatisfying, and unhealthy. Hating America damages America and damages us as well. You can hate wars, you can hate hamburgers, you can hate executions, you can hate religiosity, you can hate jazz, you can hate the idea of Sarah Palin becoming president (she won't by the way, ever) but all human beings should give America a break; should celebrate its triumphs and forgive its trespasses. That is the claim this book will make. Not, of course, in a tinny, tub-thumping, triumphalist, Fox-Newsy kind of way –because that is all over now. The election of 2008 was America's second revolution, and we need to do what even George III eventually managed to do all those years ago after the last revolution: accept it, live with it, *suck it up*.

This is a book about America, but it is not about my America. It is not a jolly romp through 50 states, a personal reminiscence of journeys taken and big characters with big hats met along the way. It is intended to be reportage, but with a twist: I do believe that the United States has been desperately misunderstood in recent years and I believe as well that much of that misunderstanding – misunderestimation as George Bush might have put it – stems from a failure of the outside world to make an effort to get to grips with a nation that seems on the face of it to be so accessible, so comprehensible, so in our faces. It is not. I want to suggest to reasonable people that the time has come – early in the Obama era – to take another look at what makes America tick. And along the way I want to take a look as well at what makes anti-Americans tick. If you love

America, and this love has dared not speak its name in recent years, this book is intended to give you ammunition with which to do battle on behalf of the yanks, not just Obama, but the nation he represents. Including that part of the nation that voted against him. And if you hate America, or think that you might, or have a friend who does, please at least give me a chance to change your mind.

Let us begin by despatching George Bush with one of the better jokes told at his expense. Bush is confiding with his senior team some time after the French have made it clear they are not going to go along with the Iraq war. He is holding forth on how pitiful France's contribution to the world has been in recent years, and it is not just their military failure he points out; they have also failed to show global economic leadership: "They don't even have a word for entrepreneur!"

I think it was a joke. But it might, of course, have been true. These have been tough times for those who want to paint a picture of America as a land of open-faced opportunity, a land which respects the rights and the achievements of other lands, takes a healthy interest in them, and leads the world in making life for everyone more comfortable, more productive, and more fun. The fact that Sarah Palin might have been elected, convinced many Europeans that America was somehow flawed, soft in the head. This book makes the case that Mrs Palin is the past. Americans' rejection of her – by large margins, they calmly decided she was unfit to be vice president – was in some ways more significant than their choice of Barack Obama.

And I want to try to convince you that America has always been, in its heart, in its soul, Obama's nation, not Palin's. The 2008 presidential campaign will of course go down in history and all of us who had anything to do with it will consider ourselves lucky to have been in America to see it buck and kick and shimmy and gallop its way to the finishing line. But this is not a book about politics. It is a book about the nation that offered up the 2008 choices, the nation that is more capable than any other on earth of noticing a problem – any problem – and acting to put it right.

Even Margaret Drabble seems to half believe that America's heart might be in the right place. But here's a warning. There is no "other America". The 2008 election represents a HUGE change of course. Even if those hoping for foreign policy U-turns are disappointed, there is no doubt that the priorities and concerns of many Americans will be very different in the post-Bush age. But anti-Americans who think they have won, that America will now see the error of its ways and become more European, are in for a rough few years. As they say in America, *good luck with that!* Instead of hoping that they become more like us, I want to suggest that we meet them halfway and in doing so challenge some of the basic pretexts of the anti-American case.

Listen to the *Today Programme* on Radio Four. Who gets the blame for most of what is wrong with Britain? Who is asked to intervene? Who is asked to resign? It's the Minister, stupid; the Government. In America it's the community, the people. Government is seen as necessary in some circumstances but never leading the way. The involvement of the government in the financial crisis is seen as a necessary evil by Americans – but always as an *evil.* As a popular car bumper sticker has it "I love America, it's the Government I don't trust ..." In Europe, millions might harbour a more or less sneaking hope that unfettered capitalism has had its day as a result of the money meltdown: no one in America has that hope.

It is more than a decade since the *Guardian* journalist Jonathan Freedland suggested that we *Bring Home the Revolution.* His book was subtitled *The Case for a British Republic* but the guts of the work was really the case for America. It was described at the time as the political book of the moment. Well, the moment came and was not seized. New Labour came and (arguably) went – Blair and Bush came and went – but the sullen British popular take on the United States as a purveyor of all that is fatty and unwholesome and militaristic and cloth-eared and generally low grade, persisted. I asked Freedland to give a ten-years-on assessment of the impact of his ideas and his response was interesting; on devolution and some other structural changes, he thought the UK had caught up with America, but on the culture question (the fundamental differences between them and us) he was clear:

That sense that Americans believe they are masters of

their own destiny, responsible for their own country, town, village etc, that sense is still largely missing in Britain. It's better than it was – there is more of a can-do culture, partly fostered by the cult of business and enterprise etc – but the semi-feudal passivity remains, I fear. You see it in the habit of looking upward, waiting for those in charge to sort things out."

My interest is not in Britain – it is in telling the story of *American* freedom, in that American self-belief that Freedland identified and eulogised ten years ago and still recognizes today, even after Bush. I want to set out the case not that America is superior, but that its obvious (and much reported) faults are counterbalanced by some less obvious (and under-reported) strengths.

America is, truth be told, a pretty weird nation in many respects. It is not the slightest bit like Europe. We have heard much in recent times about the rift between Europe and the US under George Bush, and how that rift may or may not be reduced. But the surprise is that the Atlantic is as narrow as it is; although until recently the smarter American set continued to claim some European heritage, they have truly left it behind. George Bush was a deeply un-European President it is true; but he is culturally closer to even the most bohemian San Franciscan than any citizen of the EU could ever be. In spite of ourselves, and in spite of all the evidence, we keep expecting Americans to come to their senses and have a National Health Service or a ban on keeping pistols under suburban pillows, or affection for public transport. But guys, they won't! Even under Barack Obama.

This book is about why they won't and why it doesn't matter. It is not primarily about politics. It is about human beings (us and them) and geography. The first step towards understanding America is to buy a map, preferably one with a little topography. Of course, there is more than one huge country in the world and more than one nation with mountains and deserts and plains and seashores. There are plenty of countries where the weather matches the extremes of size. But in these other places there is still a real acceptance, at home and abroad, that the effects of geography on the inhabitants will be brutal, and brutalizing. America is unique in being a leading first-world nation with third-world geography and weather. It is still possible to be crushed to death in America by debris hurled by a tornado; every year people do. It is still possible here to go off the beaten track in a state park and starve or freeze to death; again, every year people do. And for those who manage to hold on to life here – and let's face it, most of the 300 million are coping rather well – there is still a huge range of existences you can choose, a range that reaches from the most mundane and unadventurous of suburban lifestyles, to the wackiest lonesome idyll, stuck miles up a dirt track on the side of a mountain boiling your water because you think the Government is poisoning it. The possibility of achieving this kind of freedom and the *desire* to achieve it is created by geography. It is American Geofreedom. OK, there are one

17

or two people who manage eccentric existences in the UK or Belgium, or perhaps Finland, and alright, I grant you that Australia is reasonably advanced and reasonably rough, but no other advanced nation has quite this space and physical geography. Americans can seem a rather brutal lot sometimes, but this brutality is explicable and immutable; it is created at least in part by the physical fact of where they live and what that environment has done to them.

America has been a rather successful nation. Even the anti-Americans accept that it's progressed from a standing start to become, in a little over 200 years, the richest and most powerful force the world has ever seen. Yes, the land was full of natural resources, yes, a lot of it was nicked from the Indians, and yes, the early manufacturing successes were created on the backs of slaves. But the anti-Americans do not see – or consciously avert their eyes from – the history of how America was turned into a land of plenty, how it all came to be. The rest of the world has become used to American power, and forgotten that this power was earned. Yes, earned. Americans worked hard to get where they are. They did not inherit their prosperity, they invented it. Others suffered to help create it but (here we go again) our European wealth also owes much to conquest and plunder. So does the wealth of the Islamic world, such as it is. Only the Yanks get the blame.

And the blame is ceaseless. America is wealthy and powerful, the anti-Americans concede, but only to sniff at the gaudy excesses that come from too much wealth and too much power. They see Wall Street with the hedge fund managers (until recently) so overpaid. They see Main Street in Kansas with the fatties waddling around, sipping over-sized sodas. They see the freedom all Americans have to turn off to the outside world because it is not there –physically not there – unless you live on the northern or southern bor-der which not many Americans do. (Do the citizens of Russia's equivalent of Kansas City, Novosibirsk in Siberia, give a fig about the GDP of Tanzania? I doubt it, but we would never blame them for not caring)

No comparable area of the world has contributed so much to the modern economy, nor (and these points of course are linked) has any comparable area seen such a huge influx of immigrants in such a short time. The British author and journalist Harold Evans has written about the ability – in scale at least, the unique ability – of Americans to translate good ideas into practical things that make life better for large numbers of people. Many of the inventions he lists in his book *They made America* were actually made abroad or by foreigners, but it was America that allowed them to flower, to take shape, to be given practical applica-tion. America has been a place where inventors have been able to take chances, to make money; not to dream but to *do*. Among the many inventions and innovations Evans examines (the Colt revolver, the steamship, the sewing machine, the telegraph, blue jeans, vulcanized rubber, Google, etc etc), there is space for the little-known fact that the very idea of giving individuals credit ratings was invented in America: credit ratings that enabled them to borrow money to use all these things, to enjoy them – or the leisure they created – and to build more.

And along the way, this American industry and inventiveness created much of the prosperity of the rest of the world as well, through an adherence to free trade, to the commercial imperative, and to a willingness to shed blood and invest resources in keeping the planet's trading arteries unclogged. It is telling that Alan Greenspan, the former long-time boss of the Federal Reserve Bank, let slip in his memoirs that the invasion of Iraq in 2003 was about oil, or at least in his opinion should have been. Saddam was a threat to supply, and thus a threat to an entire way of life. So he had to go; the Bush team pooh-poohed such a misreading of their loftier intentions but Greenspan may well have been right.

The Cold War was another example of an American social service directed at the world. Yes, there were excesses, the support for dictators (*he may be a son of a bitch but he's our son of a bitch*) of McCarthyism, and other domestic and foreign idiocies and cruelties done in the name of anticommunism. But the winning of the Cold War was a service to humanity, every bit as vital as the US contribution to World War II. Belgium didn't win it. Neither did Britain; remember even Mrs Thatcher was ambivalent about the reunification of Germany. America pushed for freedom, not always cleverly or subtly or sensitively, but it pushed, and the fact that your Polish plumber is living a life unimaginably richer than his parents' is down to the USA. America has repeatedly saved us all from something worse than America. In this era, albeit in a ham-fisted and two-steps-forward-and-one-back kind of a way, America is performing the same service. You can of course choose to believe that the United States created all the problems of the modern world, including the rise of Islamic fascism (support for Israel, arming of the Mujahaddin in Afghanistan, support for autocrats in Arab nations, etc etc) but this is the road to madness. People who slaughter people in the name of religion are responsible for their own actions. To blame the victims of 9/11 for the crime is trite and lazy. America has certainly been responsible for some of the problems it faces around the globe – most educated Americans know that only too well – but historically this nation has created solutions and shone a beacon of light when much of the world was kicking up problems and sitting in the dark. It can – after Bush – do it again.

So what is there to dislike about America? Plenty of course.

The suburbanisation of mainstream American culture has done terrible damage to the feistiness of the place, which must surely have existed out west in days of yore. And added to this, the Puritan heritage plays havoc with American's relationship with sex. Even though the social conservatives are being put to the sword (in a wonderful example – of which more later – of America's ability to surprise and wrong-foot those who make pronouncements about its future), the fact that gay sex is still such a big deal here is decidedly odd to most civilized outsiders.

America has also had, in recent years, a problem with rationality. In *Bring Home the Revolution*, Freedland devotes only a small effort to exploring the dotty religious side to American life, but in the years since he wrote, the pervasiveness and the salience of religion have hugely increased. It will be an important part of this book. Some religions and some religious people co-exist happily with the world of scientific knowledge. This is not news in most corners of the civilized world. Well it is news, in modern America. Americans have an ability to convince themselves that believing complete tripe is perfectly fine if it has a religious patina attached. They have mistaken, as one commentator put it, the respect for religion demanded by the constitution, *with a respect for all views dressed up as religious.* I do not seek to airbrush away the dottiness of many Americans. This is a land of crazy preachers: always has been. And there has been a religious revival in recent years that has done nothing for rational thought. But my case is a more positive one: that the election of 2008 showed that the dotty brigades are on the defensive – remember this was the election that replaced the only Western leader who did not accept evolution ("the jury is out", President Bush used to say) with a contest between two leaders who did. Part of the meaning of 2008 is America pulling back from the brink of a descent into anti-rationalism. When Mr Obama swore the oath of office for the second time (after the inauguration ceremony had been messed up by the Chief Justice John Roberts), he did not use a bible. The White House staff couldn't find one and they knew perfectly well that it was not necessary for the oath to be legal.

But these are laughably minor issues, I hear you scream! What about the human sacrifices? Or at least the racial politics, the inequality, the car-obsessed baseness of so much American life? What about the hamburgers? What about the depressing addiction of Americans to guns at home and militarism abroad? Some of these issues I will address; save the human sacrifice one which, for any Americans reading, was a joke. And that reminds me of another issue: no irony. I will get to that too.

Any book about America must touch on the impact of 9/11. The American feminist thinker Susan Faludi wrote one of the more interesting early commentaries:

> In the persons of its first responders, its volunteers, and even its commuters turned combatants on a hijacked aeroplane, America had ample paragons of courage. But the national frenzy to apotheosise those people suggested a deep cultural unease beneath the hero worship; the culture lofted them into some ridiculously gilded firmament while, at the same time, dissatisfied with their example, it kept searching for more available chests to decorate with war medals.

America is troubled. Economically of course, but at a deeper psychological level as well. And the near fetishistic attitude of many Americans towards military people, military things, and military solutions, seems sometimes to be a sign of an inner malaise. I do not deny it. Many Americans would accept it.

So we need to help America by engaging with her and engaging with her people. Sniffily believing (hoping?) that the whole American system is going down the tubes is a road to mutual failure. My case is the case for rallying round, letting recent bygones be bygones, and for taking ownership of the United States, taking pride as fellow human beings in the greatest social experiment the globe has seen, an experiment of huge importance to all of us. An experiment we own.

America allows us to surprise ourselves. We do not always like what we do when we become American. We sometimes wish we could change course and be gloomier and more interesting again, or more culturally ambitious or just plain thinner. But America is still where we really want to go. Nobody wants to be Russian (other than Russians and some of them don't seem too keen) or Chinese or even European in the sense of wanting to adopt the identity of Chinese-ness of European-ness. This is not because they have nothing to offer. Plenty of the world's citizens would be better off living among these great driving forces of world history. Plenty try very hard to get there; particularly, of course, to Europe. But the dream is still the United States. Rather than acknowledging that fact in our usual grudging way *(it's where the money is*, or *it's where the space is)* we foreigners should, it seems to me, be big enough to celebrate it and understand that this fact of American attractiveness is not some strange quirk, inexplicable and best glossed over; they are telling us something, the huddled masses. More than 55 million people have chosen to move to America in the 400 years since that move became possible. Millions of them faced terrible journeys in which entire families were in peril. Many still do… America is attractive in a way no other nation has ever matched. Why then do so many foreigners persist in disliking America, misunderstanding it, trashing it?

Because we do not – or will not – understand it. And we do not – or will not – understand the driving forces of our dislike. I am not arguing that Obama is irrelevant, but I am asking that we concentrate our affection less on the man adn more on the nation that elected him. We should bite on the hamburger and notice that it tastes, as my children would say, "real good".

1. Geofreedom

The land was ours before we were the land's.
She was our land more than a hundred years
Before we were her people. She was ours
In Massachusetts, in Virginia,
But we were England's, still colonials,
Possessing what we still were unpossessed by,
Possessed by what we now no more possessed.
Something we were withholding made us weak
Until we found out that it was ourselves
We were withholding from our land of living,
And forthwith found salvation in surrender.
Such as we were we gave ourselves outright
(The deed of gift was many deeds of war)
To the land vaguely realizing westward,
But still unstoried, artless, unenhanced,
Such as she was, such as she will become.

"The Gift Outright" by Robert Frost,
read at the inauguration of John Kennedy, 1961

"I CAN'T BELIEVE this place."

The speaker is my wife, Sarah, who from day one of our adventure here has been a fan of America, an enthusiastic

27

settler, but whose frustration on this occasion has boiled over. It's four in the morning and we have just been woken by what felt like a huge explosion; the kind of disruption of the Washington suburbs of which Osama bin Laden must dream. But it wasn't him. An inspection reveals the cause of the bang and some buzzing aftershocks was an electrical power junction precariously placed on top of a pole under a large tree. In torrential rain and high winds, bits of the tree appear to have shorted the wires. The only time I have seen similar electrical arrangements was in the black South African township of Soweto outside Johannesburg during the days of apartheid, where the locals used to hook up their own wires to the junction boxes in order to enjoy free power from their white oppressors. In the rain, these unofficial electrical contrivances would look rather pretty as they fizzed and sparked, but I don't think anyone ever claimed they were particularly safe, and it was a surprise to find not dissimilar sights in the capital of the wealthiest nation on earth.

But America is eight parts rich, industrialised superpower and two parts cowboy frontier town. There is a rough edge to life here that separates the US from other wealthy places. As my seven-year-old son Sam put it, shortly after we had returned from a camping trip in West Virginia, "America is rich, right? But it doesn't look it."

It doesn't look it for a whole host of reasons – many of them linked to geography: to the open spaces and the danger that lurks in them or passes over them, or even, on occasion, lies in wait under them. There are bears in American woods: not many, perhaps a few thousand out of the 50,000 there probably were before the white settlers arrived, but still enough to get the occasional human attacked and killed, enough to make camping in the American West a different experience from camping in, say, Devon. Enough to make America similar in some respects to nations that on the face of it could hardly be more different. I read some years ago that the deputy mayor of the Indian capital Delhi had been killed by a horde of wild monkeys, which had attacked him outside his home. To an English eye, the wildness of parts of Delhi is strikingly alien; to an American, less so. To my knowledge, monkey attacks are rare in the US and attacks involving any wild animals in cities are almost unheard of, but the fact is that the idea of a wild creature coming across a human and doing him harm is not out of the way in the American psyche. It could happen; in reasonably recent memory, it used to happen a lot.

But wild animals are only a minor issue compared with the meteorological and geophysical threats with which many Americans have to cope. In our first year in Washington we had two small tornados; a hurricane which uprooted thousands of trees, damaged hundreds of houses and left us without electricity for a week; an earthquake (4.5 on the Richter scale); a plague of tree-eating cicadas; snow; intense body-sapping humid heat; and countless more minor natural disturbances. No wonder Americans are a bit rough round the edges – they need to be. Even in the capital city, a place many Americans regard as effete to the point of girliness. This nation is a tough neighbourhood. And the natural environment has helped to mould a political and social culture which – for better or for worse – can seem unpolished to the European eye. Life is not as precarious as it was for the Pilgrim Fathers or indeed the Native Americans who already lived here, but a measure of the harshness they faced is still very much a part of local American experience. We Europeans do not always understand that. There are no hurricanes in Europe. (Oh, alright, there was one in 1987, of which more later.) No tornados. (No, not real ones.) The heat is less intense and less sapping. The cold is less bone numbing. The Venus and Mars distinctions that are sometimes made between Americans and Europeans do not simply spring from nowhere. They are rooted in geography.

The physical dangers first: America doesn't look rich because much of this nation is really hanging on to its place in the first world, battling against furious and ever-present opposition from Mother Nature. I had a friend who was an airline pilot in Europe; his biggest ambition was to move to the US because, as he put it, "the weather is more interesting". Frequent fliers here will readily confirm that fact, though they find it less compelling as a reason to live on this side of the Atlantic. The fact is that America's natural environment can be very interesting. It kills people, sometimes in large numbers. Tornado shelters are a feature of the Midwest; you think little of them in rural areas where everything still looks like the set from *The Wizard of Oz* (before it gets psychedelic), but when you see them in more up-to-date settings, in the shining steel structure of Denver Airport, for instance, you realise that nature here is untamed and incapable of being tamed. The author Antonya Nelson has written of her native Kansas:

> In the centre of the country, the Kansan is aware of the vast span of time and space just outside the window. The world out there that insists an individual is just too tiny... to matter in the least.

True, Kansans live at the epicentre of America's tornado activity and there are plenty of Americans who have never seen a shelter, let alone had to rush to one, but this land is still their land. Americans have built their nation in the teeth of a storm. And the storm is never quite over. This was a recent item in an American newspaper, hardly more than filler:

> A blinding sandstorm that caught drivers by surprise caused a 12-car pileup Tuesday on a highway in the high desert north of Los Angeles, killing at least two people and injuring 16.

A lunchtime sandstorm that reduced visibility to zero – interesting weather.

And after these storms, the natural environment is always

able to cover its tracks and ours; the adventurer Steve Fossett disappeared in 2007 in a small plane over the desert in Nevada. Disappeared! They didn't find him and they gave up looking, though while the search was still on they found several other wrecks they didn't even know about. His turned up a full year later: some wreckage and some bones. This would not happen in Somerset. So forget for a moment that San Francisco sleeps every night, perched on a faultline which could lead at any moment to a catastrophic earthquake. Put Hurricane Katrina to one side. In fact, disregard all the recent news of large-scale geological and meteorological threats and potential threats. In daily life, in large swathes of America, people still look at the sky and wonder.

In the rest of the advanced world, by and large, they don't have to. We certainly don't in Britain, where the twentieth anniversary of the great storm of 1987 was celebrated with special TV programmes and reminiscences from those involved. A brush with the weather was all it was – a weak hurricane and a chance to bash Michael Fish. Another brush with the weather – the great snow of 2009 – closed London and caused such excitement on the BBC News Channel that they brought Mr Fish back in to talk about it. That same week, 50 people died in ice storms in the American Midwest. They have to be made of sterner stuff.

And that is the point. Before I lived here, I could never quite understand why Americans seemed so coarse, so untouched by the civilisation I took for granted at home.

How could they accept practices like execution, or long prison sentences for minor crimes, or gun ownership or indeed war, all of them things sophisticated Europeans have more or less left behind?

The best part of a decade spent here has lifted the scales from my eyes. I get it now, and we all could, if we would only focus on the causes of the harshness of American practices and the American way. The weather I have mentioned. When it comes to American disregard for the outside world, to that famous American ignorance about where Pakistan is on a map, or whether the United Kingdom is a Gulf Arab nation, size also matters. It really is a very long way from sea to shining sea. Even Americans get confused about the extent of their dominion: a magazine in New Mexico used to publish a regular feature entitled "one of our 50 is missing!" Readers would send in examples of organisations in other states wondering where exactly New Mexico might be and occasionally asking about the need for visas.

But ignorance of their own country is one thing; again and again anti-Americans complain about the attitude of Americans towards the rest of the world, about the insularity of American life, about the percentage of Americans who have passports or have been to Vladivostok or speak fluent Swahili. Yet outsiders – particularly Europeans – often have only the vaguest idea of where Kansas is, or Rhode Island, or indeed New Mexico. And how many British people – proud owners of passports – actually use them only to travel to France or Spain, the equivalent of a jaunt from

Chicago to South Carolina, to get some sun and pop home? Americans don't need passports (until recently they didn't need them to go abroad either to Canada or the Caribbean). That is why they don't have them. To use the passport argument to suggest that Europeans are somehow keener explorers of the world is simply wrong. Of course, plenty of us are woefully ignorant of our fellow human beings, but the ignorance of Americans is held up as evidence of their hopeless inadequacy, while the rest of us are free to see the United States as New York, San Francisco and a blur of nameless places in between. It is like the difference between knowledge of the humanities and knowledge of applied science. You can be ignorant about how a light bulb works but still cut it in polite society if you know what Proust was getting at. Similarly among the sophisticates of the world, a knowledge of the geography of Europe (where is Lichtenstein?) counts for a lot more than similar knowledge about the United States. Where is Nebraska? Don't care.

Should care, I say. But why? Well, as with the weather and the geology, American space gives clues about the formation of the American character. These are not get-out-of-jail cards for badly behaved presidents (Oh, you'll have to forgive him, he's from Texas, or pretends to be) but they are pointers towards greater knowledge of the American soul. We bend over backwards to know why "the Arab street" thinks as it does; in the case of America we should be equally curious to look for causes, wellsprings, beginnings.

So luxuriant was the growth of the ten thousand year old forest that covered all but a few scattered portions of it – a forest that had developed after the retreat of the last Ice Age in North America – that mariners coming from Europe in the late spring or early summer were greeted while still at sea, far from the sight of land, by the mingled scent of sun-warmed resins from millions of pines and cedars and fragrance of myriad flowering shrubs and trees.

John Harmon McElroy, in his book *American Beliefs* sets a scene that takes the breath away. It certainly gave pause to the early settlers, and as I note later on, some of them pronounced such fecundity a touch overwhelming and probably not desperately conducive to civilised life. And it is true that for European gentlefolk it was not an easy place to live, this Stone Age vastness, this interminable and some-times hostile wilderness. Many of the early European settlers starved because they simply could not put the place to work. But in time they managed, and managed hugely well. America's story has been the story of the conquest of the continent. As McElroy puts it:

The continuous transformation of the great wilderness of forest, prairie, plains, mountains, and desert that once stretched across the entire centre of the world's third largest continent… has been the principal event in the history of the American people. The behaviours and consequences associated with that transformation have, directly and indirectly, shaped many of the beliefs of American culture.

It is worth adding that modern scholarship has convincingly over-ridden the idea that "the great wilderness" was entirely empty of people and, more crucially, of civilisation. A convincing case can be made – and is explored in Charles C. Mann's *1491* – that some of the rugged individualism of the American character comes directly from the organisation and social mores of Native American society, in particular from the loose confederacy of tribes and nations making up the Haudenosaunee ("People Building a Long House") who had successfully put an end to Stone Age tribal warfare long before the white men arrived. And in doing so had begun some of the traditions of which modern America is so proud. Mann quotes a seventeenth-century Jesuit complaining, "All these barbarians have the law of wild asses – they are born, live, and die in liberty without restraint; they do not know what is meant by bridle and bit".

Indeed. And many early settlers went off to live in these attractive conditions or lived so close to them that they became infected – particularly with what appears to have been the Indian lack of respect for social class and inherited authority.

But Native Americans and settlers alike had to do battle with the elements, with nature. This fight has left its mark. There is a strong belief, even in the modern nation, in the duty of all Americans to grapple with nature. The people who starved when they arrived here in the early seventeenth century tended to be the nobility. A belief in the almost sacred value of hard work, and of the rights of families to profit from hard work, surely began in those early frightening, coruscating winters. The earliest settlers brought with them the mores and practices of the Old World, of course, in particular the idea of indentured servitude, where a person had to "pay off" the cost of the passage with years of free labour. But even these people were soon better off than they had been at home. The per capita income of Americans in the years before the revolution was already higher than that of English people. America had already taken off before 1776. It had taken only a few years for the early settlers to realise that private property, widely owned, encouraged industry. Europeans, with their feudal system and the cultural baggage that surrounded it, with their tightly monitored villages and their strict hierarchies, had taken twenty times as long to civilise their continent. Some Europeans still don't get it.

But the driving force behind this American approach was not, and is not, some abstract academic belief in individualism. The idea that birth rank was irrelevant, that dukes were a joke if they could not till fields, that aristocratic titles were cute and fascinating but not directly relevant to everyday life, that social order needed to be efficient and conducive to maximum production and use of talents; they did not read this stuff in a book, or at least not until Milton Friedman arrived on the scene. American individualism springs directly from the need of the early Americans – including Native Americans – to survive and prosper and do it quickly. They chose what worked, in terms of social organisation and overarching ethic: hard work, everyone involved, and everyone able to benefit. They had space to parcel up and hand out, and that of course meant that huge numbers of ordinary people could own land; it also meant in time that millions of ordinary people were not part of a huge pool of labour for hire. Labour was expensive and wages were high.

The abundance of land also meant that people could avoid even the relatively light touch of authority in American townships and settlements; there was nobody to supervise you, no nobleman to respect, no church you were forced to join, no rigid structure holding you back. The result was a mental freedom, caused and sustained by the geography, which continues to this day.

The geography of America, and the opportunities and risks faced by the early settlers, is also responsible I think for the stunning, the unique, the shining example of American giving. Americans are the most generous people on earth. They give staggering sums of money: \$229 billion was donated by individuals in 2007 according to Giving USA, an organisation that monitors charity and the charitable sector. Is this simple altruism? No, of course it isn't. Those American settlers who forged ahead into the wilderness all those years ago were wonderfully free but also horribly unprotected. They had to look after themselves and they had to combine with each other to do it; they learned the value of individualism and the cost of isolationism all wrapped up in one lesson. So they gave their time and their money for the common good. Unprotected by government, they sorted out their own solutions. And they still do. So American giving is often giving aimed at oneself and one's family. Even such limited generosity is something we Brits find culturally alien. An example: there is an American private school I have been told about, a multinational place outside which the flags of the various nationalities in attendance proudly hang. Save one. The Union Jack is not there. British children attend the school. British mums and dads pick them up and drop them off. But there is no flag. Why not? Well, the parents are meant to pay. The school will arrange to buy the flag but the parents must cough up the funds. The British parents, being British, think they pay plenty in fees already and have no desire to come up with the cash. Americans are horrified by this. I told the story once and an American in the audience (he was a cameraman, not poor but not super-rich) came up to me afterwards with a cheque book and offered to donate the requisite sum. The point is that Americans believe in self-help. They believe in charitable giving to prop up the comforts of everyday life. They give huge sums to foreign charities, it is true, and to disaster relief at home and abroad, but most of the cash is going towards the enrichment of their own existences.

On March 25th, 1745, ten men executed pledges totalling £185 "for the purpose of Erecting a Collegiate School in the province of New Jersey for the instructing of youth in the Learned Languages, Liberal Arts, and

Sciences". Today, Princeton University's endowment is worth $14 billion. No British university, however much more ancient and venerable, can come close. And that money has been given, in the most part, by grateful former students. Students who feel themselves to be part of a private community just as their forebears did. De Tocqueville noticed it: in France and England he wrote, associations were formed generally from the top down – governments or "upper-class" people would organise them and run them and sustain them. In eighteenth-century America however, "Americans of all ages, all conditions, all dispositions constantly form associations". They still do: and the reason they do, and the reason they fund them as well as they do, is again not the result of some academic commitment to the free market and charity as opposed to socialism and state dependency. The reason is to be found in the geography, in the need for self-reliance tempered by social responsibility that the early settlers grappled with and grasped. When President Obama tries to persuade Americans to volunteer and take part in their communities and their lives he pushes on an open door, a door opened by history but more importantly by geography. When it was first inhabited the space was ungovernable in the old fashioned sense: new forms of association and new ways of thinking were necessary for the great experiment to take flight.

There is still space in the USA. Room to run. And I am not talking about the Great Plains. Ten minutes outside Washington DC – really, ten minutes – you can be in a wilderness overlooking the Potomac River with not a house, not a human being in sight. This is not the case in London or Paris or Rome or Berlin. And if you fall into the Potomac, into the rushing water at Great Falls, for instance, just a few minutes' drive out of DC, you are on your own. As you drown, you would see the airliners dipping down overhead to land at Reagan National Airport. You would know that you were very close to the levers of US power and the monuments to US might. But you would die nonetheless. America's physical environment breeds rugged individualism – the longer I live here, the more I see a causal link between the width of the place, its extent and its topography, and its mindset. Part of it is atavistic: or at least grounded in the experience of the early settlers who became landowners and land tamers on a scale never before seen in human history. But it is a mistake to assume that modern America – comfortable, slothful, suburban America – is so hugely different. Access to wilderness is not limited, as it is in Britain, to country folk or those who can afford a second home in the Lake District – cheap petrol (by European standards) and plenty of space combine to make this a nation of amateur explorers, conquerors of nature. You can load up the truck and ship out of town, any American town, and be lost before dusk. And when you get there you can get wild.

An example: I am in an opencast coal mine in West Virginia, the guest of a private mine owner who wants to publicise the benefits of coal as the fuel of the future. The chief benefit, truth be told, is that there is plenty of it left in the ground. This being a land of efficiency as well as a land of space, the mine owners take a very direct route to the seams of potential fuel: they blow the tops off the mountains. Europeans will shudder at the environmental wantonness of this activity (and many Americans do as well) but it does bring home to you the fact that this nation is chock-full of mountains, and the loss of a few peaks hardly registers on the national radar. I am musing on this fact – and pulling on some boots for the hike around what's left of this particular mountain – when I notice an unnerving fact: several of the drivers of those super-sized mechanical diggers they favour in the macho world of the opencast pit are packing heat. The truck drivers have large guns – hunting rifles – pointing out of their cabs; they look like extras in some dark post-nuclear drama. In fact the men are hunters enjoying the first day of the deer season – the mine owner improved morale by allowing his employees to take pot shots from their vehicles before they knocked off for the day. It's all very brutal – very dangerous – *but* here's the deal in the land of the free: if it is on private land, you can get away with it. You have to wear a red vest so that your buddy doesn't wing you but that appears to be the only rule.

What I witnessed in West Virginia was the coming together of two important traditions. First, that ordinary men (and women, I suppose, though not in West Virginia) have the right to carry weapons and kill animals – hunting in America is not the preserve of sherry-quaffing posh folk. Secondly, that on private property you can do your thing. An Englishman's home is his castle, we Brits used to say, but always in the knowledge that the castle was usually small, overlooked and surrounded by security cameras. In West Virginia, homes are often far from being castles. Often homes are trailers parked by the side of the road. But around them they have what the best castles have always had: plenty of space. Space to go crazy and kill animals.

Space as well to enslave and harm fellow human beings in a manner unimaginable in rural Yorkshire. The brutal truth is that in this area – geofreedom – as in others of American life, there is a cost. And sometimes the cost is high. In 2008, a polygamous sect – an offshoot of the Mormon Church – was accused of practices that amounted to organised child abuse. In their Texas hideaway, on private land unseen by the forces of authority, it was alleged that they organised "marriages" between elderly men and girls as young as sixteen, marriages that were then "consummated" in front of other men. Someone complained to the police, who finally raided the compound. The children, amid scenes of great hand-wringing, were taken into protective custody. In the end though the evidence did not stand up and the children were returned.   .

But hold on. The sect belongs to Warren Jeffs, who is serving two consecutive prison sentences for being an accomplice to the rape of a fourteen-year-old girl who was married to her cousin in Utah. In spite of the fact that the *leader* of the sect is plainly a child abuser, the Texas authorities held back from investigating and are now in trouble (accused of unconstitutional behaviour) for going in when they did. This community had legally bought the land on which they planted their temple. No outsider complained about them. That is geofreedom.

Which is not to say that Americans always, or even commonly, use their space for brutal and destructive pursuits. Panoramic vistas mostly enhance American life and American attitudes. And the vistas boggle the mind. Monument Valley, that quintessential cowboy-film moonscape somewhere east of the Grand Canyon in the states of Arizona and Utah, ought to be one of the great tourist destinations of the world. It is unique – the red rocks that formed the backdrop to a hundred Western films and for the iconic advertising campaign of the Marlboro Man simply do not exist in this form anywhere else on the planet. For as far as the eye can see there is nothing but baked-sand desert and the huge protuberances that ancient rivers have left standing in massive weird isolation. It is a view that stays with you for ever. But there is nobody there! Well, alright, in the height of the season there are cars on Route 163, the road that meanders past the monuments, but this is no Stonehenge. For one thing, it takes real determination to get to Monument Valley – it's a day's drive from Phoenix in Arizona or Santa Fe in New Mexico. And for another, there is just so much of it – hours and hours of space – that you never feel hemmed in. What does this do to the

American soul? How does it affect the emerging folk memory of the American people? Does it speak of possibilities rather than limitations? Does it suggest exploration and adventure, over societal values of coexistence and self-control? Does it lead to an attitude of mind that squints at the horizon? ? Did the young Barack Obama do exactly that when his mum took him on a tour of the nation by Greyhound bus?

It is certainly true that many of America's finest hours, as seen by Americans themselves, involve the conquest of natural obstacles. They are still at it, particularly out west, where a new population explosion is under way, in cities like Phoenix and Las Vegas. Vegas is, of course, uniquely odd; Phoenix has pretensions to being just a normal big city. But look at it from the air: it really should not be there. All around is the parched desert of the south-west United States – the temperature outside the cocoon of air-conditioning is regularly over 40C. But the citizens are cool and Phoenix is expanding. It is an expensively hydrated testament to modern America's can-do spirit. But it exists on a knife edge. Modern Americans gave Phoenix its name because it seemed to be rising from the ashes of a past civilisation – the Hohokam people who lived there from early times, finally dying out in the fifteenth century. The author Craig Childs has written of the fate that may await modern-day Phoenix:

When archaeologists study the Hohokam, they see a

civilization that finally collapsed under the weight of drought, overpopulation, and ensuing social disarray. When they look at Phoenix, they see potential for the same.

Now I know that the United Kingdom could in theory suffer a similar fate. Global warming could bring searing heat to Weston-super-Mare. Birmingham could... Well, something could happen to Birmingham. But Americans, for all their bluster, and for all our visions of them as over-mighty conquerors of this, that and the other, still face dangers that we do not. My parents-in-law live in Reading, in Berkshire. Reading changes over the years; employment opportunities come and go, housing estates are built and expand, inner city warehouses are done up and sold off, but none of these changes is driven by geography. Reading is where it is because three rivers meet there, but that geographical fact is no longer a driving force. There is a fetid stability in the English Home Counties that American towns do not have. In the US the towns themselves are every bit as stable – and often far uglier – but the hugeness of the nation that surrounds them invests American small-town life with a kind of edginess that most of the UK, most of Europe, cannot match.

The point of that Robert Frost poem is that Americans became American when they embraced the land: "such as we were we gave ourselves outright". Other nations grow organically over time; they are plainly shaped by the environment, but the impact is hidden or diluted by other inputs. In America the looming large of the land is a recent folk memory. Of course there is space in other nations, bad weather too, and all manner of natural hazards and propensity to calamity. Canadians – in their dozy way – have to face the odd bit of snow, though generally none of the meteorological and geological calamities of their cousins to the south. But the Canadians are a reminder that merely living in North America is not enough to create the spirit of the United States. The roughness of the neighbourhood is – as the philosophers put it – a necessary cause of American-ness, but it is not sufficient.

2. Anti-America

WHY THEN DO Europeans feel the way they do about the United States? Where does anti-Americanism come from?

It's all the fault of the French. They invented it. They did it long before McDonald's existed, or Hollywood or George W. Bush. And they did it long before socialism existed as well, long before left-wing hostility to the United States became a feature of European thought.

In fact, snooty Europeans (in fairness to the French, they were by no means the only villains) invented anti-Americanism without even waiting for America to became a nation. Years before 1776 and all that, they were hard at it. In the absence of a US government to agitate against or blame for the woes of the eighteenth century world – olive oil wars perhaps – they concentrated on that climate, that harsh and unforgiving geography I mentioned in the last chapter. Even in the early part of the eighteenth century, the prevailing view among French academics and those who moved in their circles and hung out in their salons, was that the place stank. It was – *of its very nature* – a dump. It was too humid, the philosophers and scientists pronounced, for human life to prosper. Even the dogs did not bark. One possible explanation: that a second Biblical flood had soaked the place rather recently leaving it uninhabitable for the foreseeable future. Otherwise, it was just an unfortunate fact of life that the West was not best, and never would be.

In a BBC interview for my Radio Four documentary on anti-Americanism, James Ceaser of the University of Virginia put it like this: the prevailing scientific view throughout the eighteenth century had been contemptuous of America and Native Americans and quite certain that those Europeans who travelled there had better get out quick. It was blind prejudice backed up with bad science:

> Things that were already here – for example the animals – were inferior to the animals of the old continent, and everything that came here degenerated, so that the Euro-Americans who came to the United States lost potency, sexual potency, lost intelligence. Everything on this continent was in a state of decay.

Dr Ceaser also introduces us to a feature of anti-Americanism as alive and kicking today as it was when the bewigged European thinkers were sharpening their nibs. Anti-Americanism is often linked to fear – fear nowadays of a lifestyle damaging to many of the world's more hidebound and tradition-worshiping regimes and elites, fear then that the entire population would up sticks and hop it to the New World if they had half a chance and the truth were told about the opportunities there. The most vitriolic of the denigrators of the American continent, the Dutchman Cornelius de Pauw, was in the pay of the court of Frederick the Great. Frederick was worried about emigration to America; so his servant de Pauw's anti-Americanism served a purpose, just as Hugo Chavez's anti-Americanism does today. Neutrality, over the question of America, has never existed: it is not that motives have always been base or concealed – Hugo Chavez has a point after all, if not a very convincing one – but motives are always there; America is a continent, a nation, an idea, that does not foster neutrality in the same way as, say, Iceland.

Cornelius De Pauw set to his work with some gusto and launched a ship every bit as adaptable and robust as the *Mayflower*, in fact more so, because the ship of European anti-Americanism has never been sunk. De Pauw told his wide-eyed European audiences that America was a continent "struck with putrefaction", and the effect of this natural decay on the local population was damning: "A stupid imbecility is the fundamental disposition of all Americans."

In the end, of course, the biologists' attack came up against the facts and the facts won. Yes, America was harsh, it was not a cornucopia, an innocent idyll, untouched by the traumas of the outside world, as some of the early discoverers had hoped (again, no neutrality on the American question), but nor was it noticeably hopeless. So over time, some of the early European sneers about the inherent nastiness of the place turned to muted praise and even a grudging acceptance that one day, in the long-term future, America might show promise. The Americans themselves were almost pathetically keen to do their best to defend their homeland (shades of modernity here?) with Thomas Jefferson sending most of a whole dead moose to France so that the Comte de Buffon – the greatest biologist of the age – could solemnly examine it and agree, finally, that it was indeed a rather fine animal and, *quelle horreur*, was in fact a tad larger than the European equivalents.

By the time the colonists were beginning to look just as healthy as Europeans, with their dogs barking quite normally and their potency no longer in question, the most wonderful thing began to happen. The anti-Americans shifted their ground, just as they have throughout subsequent history, in order to keep one step ahead of those difficult facts. So the natural state of the place was no longer the problem. "Although it was once laid waste," prophesied the eighteenth-century thinker the Abbé Raynal, "this new world will flourish in its time and perhaps dominate the old."

Dominate the old. Aha! No longer feeble, they are about to become domineering. But wait...

I suppose I should acknowledge that according to my grand theory of Why Americans Are Like They Are, the eighteenth-century *philosophes* had a point. They spotted very early the pitfalls of making America home. Modern anti-Americans would do well to read these tracts and wonder at the hazards, real and imaginary, that faced those who set up the nation. But Europe's nascent anti-Americans failed to spot a few things; first, that in amongst the swamps there was a superabundance of the kind of raw materials and fertile land upon which a nation could be built; the weather is dreadful at times, to be sure, but it can be wonderfully good as well. Secondly, they did not know the calibre of the native people who lived in the so-called New World, whose knowledge and wisdom would be used shamelessly by the early settlers. And thirdly, they could not know of the calibre of those settlers, in particular of the Europeans who made the dangerous journey to Plymouth Rock in spite of the horrors prophesied by those who claimed to be in the know.

And once those settlers had got themselves going and for a hundred years or so built their nation and prospered, it was time for the European tune to change; time for the beginning of the transformation of the Euro-whine from a concentration on the salty swampiness of the landscape to a complaint about the altogether uncalled-for confidence and bluster of these ghastly upstart Americans, and the threat they posed to everyone else.

Maybe the appeal of the anti-American accordion tune, the key to its longevity, is the uncanny knack it has of getting both the left and the right foot tapping. Bernard-Henri Lévy, French intellectual and all-round upper-crust commentator, puts it like this:

> Anti-Americanism historically, genealogically, comes from the fascist tendency in French thought. Anti-Americanism is based on the fear, on the hatred of democracy... The French extreme right has an enemy... Which is the idea of people coming from every origin, deciding to form a nation.

This, surely, is the central pillar in the anti-American edifice. It is the hatred, sometimes conscious, sometimes subliminal, of the idea of a nation built from scratch, without common ties of blood, without common roots, without common ethnic heritage. It is the visceral fear of the melting pot, of which Barack Obama is only the most famous example, but by no means the most exotic. And on that visceral fear, a mighty empire of contempt has been spawned. Bernard-Henri Lévy's point is that this virus, having begun on what we would nowadays call the far right, has had the ability to circulate effortlessly through the body politic and turn up, slightly altered, but fundamentally similar, on the left side.

You can almost feel the migration taking place in the pages of the brilliant de Tocqueville classic *American Democracy*, published in 1848 but still *the* text for a basic understanding of how the place ticks. De Tocqueville had plenty of time for the United States, and unlike many of its detractors, took time to get to know it before passing comment. Much of what he saw, he approved of. But on the subject of the baleful effects of democracy on American cultural mores, he was pretty uncompromising and his views fast became the norm: "In aristocracies a few great pictures are produced; in democratic countries a vast number of insignificant ones. In the former, statues are raised of bronze; in the latter, they are modeled in plaster."

The aristocratic political take on America was joined in the twentieth century by a wider cultural attack. Even Adolf Hitler got in on the act: the remark that "A single Beethoven symphony contains more culture than America ever created" is attributed to him.

Bernard-Henri Lévy tells us the next step in the migration of this notion, this anti-democratic virus, is to the left of the body politic, and it is easy to find examples of the process he describes: one of the most telling was this commentary from Hubert Beuve-Méry, the man who founded *Le Monde* – an organ of the left – in May 1944. "The Americans," he said, "represent a real danger for France, different from the one posed by Germany or the one with which the Russians may in time threaten us: the Americans may have preserved the cult of liberty, but they do not feel the need to liberate themselves from the servitude their capitalism has created."

The virus invades the left. But even then it does not stay still. It adapts with the times, hops from cause to cause. Euro-communism is not fashionable any more – but European opposition to globalisation is the cause of the hour. The European anti-Americans are there. Never mind that French companies compete on the world stage and in world markets and seek to do so efficiently and without national boundaries getting in the way. Americans do it more and do it better, and get all the blame. In particular, because American companies are so successful – because American ideas are so successful – they get the blame for the horrible fact of worldwide homogenisation; for the unbearable notion that people around the world might get what they want and might want roughly the same things. In the same packets. With the same sauce. American sauce.

To unearth the modern-day anti-Americans, I went to Paris. There is nowhere better for a demonstration. On a wonderful spring day, I attended a huge and good-natured get-together, with a unicyclist leading the troops and large numbers of colourful flags and banners representing all manner of left-leaning causes and gripes. The traffic was stopped for the occasion and the cobbled streets echoed to the sounds of chanting and music. It was much louder and more ragged than the ordered little protests of my mum's friends in Bath all those years ago – the sensible shoes over thick brown stockings, the drab coats, the drizzle – but *voilá!* the same bogeyman is on everyone's minds. America!

After we had marched a mile or two, a cheer went up; the star of the show was making his way to the front. The leader of this charge, the man who embodies European-style values, long lunches and short working days, had arrived, fashionably late, to take his place at the head of the procession. José Bové once burned down a McDonald's.

His action, in the south of France at the head of another demonstration back in 1989, propelled him into a position of global leader of the anti-globalisation brigades.

Mr Bové cuts an odd figure; moustachioed and thick set, the classic French artisan look, yet surrounded on the day I met him by the modern European protest set; the hoodies, the crusties, the campaigners against this, that and the other. These folks, as President Bush might have said, are the embodiment of the connection between the modern left and the old-style, visceral haters of the effects of democracy. They hate America for left-wing reasons and for aristocratic reasons; for the perception that American trading practises damage the poor, and for the smell of the hamburger and the threat it poses to indifferent quiche served by surly smoking Parisian waiters.

I walked for a bit alongside Mr Bové and he told me that everywhere in the world when people hear the word America, they are afraid. He is not personally anti-American, he assured me; he is opposed only to America's policy mistakes. But this is a politician's answer; he dislikes what America IS, and the cheapening, as he sees it, of French culture at the hands of the behemoth to the west. Burning down a McDonald's sends a message that the early French aristocratic anti-Americans would have understood very well, as would de Tocqueville (though he would not have approved of it), Beuve-Méry and the rest. Globalisation is seen as Americanisation and that in turn is seen as homogenisation of culture, of life, of heritage. This very demonstration, this postprandial saunter through the streets, is under threat. American-style freedom of choice threatens tradition.

Of course, the view that the Americans are, fundamentally, a threat to a way of life is not unique to the Parisian street. It is a view held in the *salons* as well. Soon after my encounter with Mr Bové, I entered one of those *salons*, surrounded by exquisite furniture and attentive staff: the office of Hubert Védrine, the former Foreign Minister. Mr Védrine is very proud of his invention of a word: *Hyperpuissance*. This hyper-power is what the US possesses and this hyper-power is what the rest of the world must keep in check.

Védrine has been leading the march of the modern-day French intellectual left; his is the *salon* set as opposed to the street protesters, but they have the same target: the USA, the barbarians in Washington. Actually, he does not put it like that. What he says is less stark but nonetheless telling in its characterisation of the threat from the West:

> The American people believe that they have this special role to play and because of that they can forget all the lessons of history... In addition they are a people with a mission. They believe they have a mission to convert the whole world to democracy, to human rights, to the market economy. So it's a colonising people like the British and the French, but the British and the French have learned that it doesn't work... The Americans believe in themselves.

In the face of this attractive but dangerous friend – this kid with a gun – Védrine wants the rest of the world to club together to keep itself free. "We want to keep our independent way of thinking, our autonomy of action," he tells me, and his solution is a stronger set of international rules to contain US power. Tie the monster down.

Védrine's case is compelling. It is not couched in terms of hatred, it is not dismissive of the achievements of the United States, or the kindness of its inhabitants. It recognises American power and seeks to curtail it through rules enforced by international committees, not to attack it. It is, in many ways, the archetypal modern European way of doing battle: talk your enemy into submission. Do not finish him off – that would be vulgar – but keep him confused.

I put the Védrine plan to the man who epitomises American unilateralism, the man who once said that the United Nations did not exist, and who, when he discovered that it did, said you could take the top few stories off the building and no one would notice; the man who ended up as UN ambassador for the United States – John Bolton.

He laughed. "Good luck," he said. I persisted: "What they say is that they have a historical perspective that allows them sometimes to correct the overenthusiasm, if I can put it that way, of some people in the United States."

"You remind me why we declared our independence in the first place."

But John Bolton, fun as he was, is history. I wonder if Védrine's approach is one with which Obama's America can learn to live? After all, the limits of unilateral action were horribly exposed during the Bush years. Might a Védrine tack allow the United States to keep some of its power, but to have that power grounded once again in international legitimacy? America, after all, invented the global institutions of the post-war world. The United States promoted the global system and benefited from the stability it provided. Mr Obama's UN Ambassador has a seat in his cabinet. Perhaps Obama's America could be brought back into the fold.

Oh, but how unconfident we all are! Do we really need a formal system to hold back a power that relies for most of its oomph on attractiveness rather than oppression?

The most striking feature of the brand of anti-Americanism epitomised by the French but found elsewhere in Europe, even in the UK, is how unable it is to take the long view, to see some homogenisation as human progress, but to realise as well that in a market-driven world, there are limits to how far the American wagon can travel.

There are some things the French do wonderfully well. Sex, for instance. As I point out elsewhere in this book, the Americans haven't got a clue about it. Nobody goes to America in search of eroticism, at least I hope they don't. Trains as well are rather good in France, and almost always hopeless in the US. You can stand in the Gare de Lyon and marvel at the French system; you can hop on a TGV to Geneva or to Marseilles and they really do go fast, and they really are affordable. Go to St Louis Station in Missouri, once the greatest in the world, the gateway to the west, and you'll find a shopping mall. In America, they have abandoned their railways; in Europe they have not. We take different routes. We *can* take different routes. The United States is not a monster preventing us from living our own lives, it is not a steamroller about to crush us; American culture is fun. At the Gare De Lyon, you see kids wearing ipods (invented by an Englishman, yes, but brought to your ears by American drive and vision) but sipping *cafés au lait* and waiting for trains, rather than chugging Diet Coke and waiting for planes; good for them, I say! They celebrate a fact, that the United States is a source of opportunity but is not to be aped in every respect and does not desire to be. Individual US firms are of course rapacious and badly behaved on occasion, but companies in all nations are rapacious and badly behaved on occasion. We get back to what we might name the Bath Abbey Churchyard Fallacy, of blaming Americans for merely doing what we would all do if we had the gumption and opportunity. My visit to France coincided with the expulsion from Bolivia of a French private water company accused of overcharging the locals. They were not shouting about that on the streets of Paris. Nor do they raise their voices against Chinese companies cutting a swathe through Africa.

We British are not quite as myopic. But there are those among us who would lead us into temptation. Again, on both sides of the political divide we slip too easily into contempt for the United States, a contempt that treats

American ideas as suspect, American goods as Trojan horses from which culture killers will leap, and Americans themselves as fat ignoramuses.

Harold Macmillan's revealing view that Britain played the Greeks to America's Romans (Romans were militaristic and culturally vacuous with nasty eating habits and a penchant for bloody sports, Greeks were philosophical and invented civilised things like history) captured a mood on the right of British politics that is not a million miles from the view of John Pilger on the left. Messrs Macmillan and Pilger have, so far as I am aware, no other connection but this vision of America. Across the political divide, this jaundiced view of the New World circulates and mutates and re-emerges.

Take the subject of American television. The very phrase "American television" contains a meaning in the UK that all of us instantly cotton on to, a little cultural in-joke we can all enjoy: American television means crap. It is often to be cited in the same sentence as "repeats" – in other words, it is a sign of something having gone wrong; it is not a good thing. Throughout my life there have been complaints about it, and on and on they go; one of the latest, was a delightful re-emergence of *The Wombles of Wimbledon Common* in an effort to keep Disney at bay. A 90-second remake of the classic children's series was produced recently by a group of campaigners for British television and more generally for British culture. They called their updated show *Badass Wombles of Central Park* and gave the characters

American accents and loutish habits. This was meant to point out to dozy compliant Britons the extent of the cultural disaster at hand. These American Wombles are recognisable but foreign. When one of them is mugged (you have more chance of being mugged these days on Wimbledon Common than in Central Park but let us not quibble) the cry goes out, "Call 911!" The film ends with Bernard Cribbins making the case for "British programmes for British kids before it's too late".

The Wombles are wonderful. They are better than their American equivalents, wittier and racier and less sentimental, but the impetus for the production of future Wombles must come from us. It cannot come from whinging at the Americans. We have to find the funding and the enthusiasm, and compete with the Disney behemoth.

But what if we fail to keep the monster at bay? Well, actually, we have always failed and always benefited from that failure. This is – as a *Guardian* writer put it – "a storm in Mr Benn's teacup". In fact (Wombles apart), American TV is, whisper it softly, much better than the British variety in many respects. Look at news. CNN revolutionised the way news is gathered and disseminated around the world. It is highly America-centric but its ability to get to stories and bring them live to viewers was, for many years, unsurpassed. The BBC has a global TV news channel of its own now and a very good one it is, but I doubt it would exist if CNN had not pointed the way. In the BBC, we are calmer and steadier in our analysis of world events, but they were first to reach them.

But never mind news, look instead at the programmes most viewers watch. In their anti-American classic *Why Do People Hate America?*, Merryl Wyn Davies and Ziauddin Sardar engaged in a lengthy deconstruction of the meaning of the post-9/11 episodes of the hit series *The West Wing*. They thought the programme – an account of a fictional, left-of-centre American president – contained messages reinforcing the notion that the attacks of that day were unprovoked and illegitimate. Heaven forbid. But they missed the real story, these anti-Americans. They failed to see the fundamental achievement of *The West Wing* writers and actors; they have created a programme about America that is compelling and thought-provoking and funny and addictive – another of those famous world brands. It is true that a lot of bad US television is dumped abroad, but plenty of the good stuff is lapped up, and quite rightly. A friend of mine who worked in 10 Downing Street said he and his colleagues used to compare themselves and their roles to characters in *The West Wing*: as the nation chatters endlessly about nasty US television, the people running Britain are glued to… well, nasty US television.

And what about *24, ER, Desperate Housewives,* and from my boyhood, *MASH, Kojak* and *Starsky and Hutch*? What about the work of the playwright David Mamet whose demanding, challenging, eviscerating scripts (*Glengarry, Glenross* et al) are written at his home in lazy, commercial, sunny Santa Monica, a stone's throw from Hollywood.

True, this king of gritty dialogue has trouble getting the word "motherfucker" on mainstream TV – I am not pretending this is a medium wholly owned by the artists and their art – but the fact is that he writes for television *and* he writes for Hollywood, and he is as brilliant and coruscating a cultural critic as you will find anywhere on earth.

In spite of our so-called special relationship with the USA Brits too often see the United States as a cultural black hole. But this stuff sings: it lasts in the mind like all the best popular culture. American television can improve your health, or at least your well-being.

Bugger *The Wombles.*

And this is the crucial point: American television does not crowd out our home-grown stuff. It complements it. We are still able to create *The Office* and *Strictly Come Dancing* and *Pop Idol* and – perfidious cultural imperialists that we are – flog them across the Atlantic. American networks saw their worth and bought them. They saw Simon Cowell and realised that this rude chap would be an eye-opener in the US. Indeed he was. American audiences see the worth of these programmes and watch them. We should be proud of this two-way street, but we should accept that it is not all high quality going from us to them – the virus of reality TV was invented on the British side of the Atlantic – and poor quality coming from them to us.

Like those train travellers at the Gare de Lyon, we can choose our destination. And the lazy view of globalisation as being synonymous with Americanisation is simply wrong, it seems to me, and destined for a technologically-driven early grave. Think about it: every year, it becomes cheaper and easier for the modern-day equivalent of *The Wombles* to be made in someone's garage and sent anywhere via the internet. The internet is dominated at the moment by American users and the English language but will this be the case in 30 years? Does it have to be? If other people come up with clever attractive ideas, who in America is in a position to squelch them? There is no centrally processed game plan for US domination. Nobody could have planned it. And nobody, no president, no American organisation, however wealthy and currently powerful, will be able to map out a path to the next stage. Communication, person to person, company to company, charity to charity, drug cartel to drug cartel, terrorist to terrorist: that's the power structure of the future world. America is at the heart of many of those hubs through merit: because it is open to ideas and technology and talent. If that changes, American power will fade. To get hung up on hamburgers is to allow the obsession with the US to get in the way of rational thought.

Anti-Americanism peaked in the UK and in France at the time of the Iraq War. There was a sense of real anger, not just that President Bush had gone to war but that Americans had re-elected him and overwhelmingly backed his decision to attack Saddam Hussein. Now some of this passion was directed against policy rather than against a people. It cannot properly be counted as anti-Americanism, any more than criticism of Israel is anti-Semitic. But my point is that the Iraq war is not – as is sometimes suggested – the sole or principal cause of anti-American feeling in Western Europe; a tweak in foreign policy will not lead to sweetness and light.

The tweak is at hand in the Obama presidency. But the sweetness and light will only come if the Europeans relax, and having relaxed, address some of the fundamental issues separating us from them. We have atavistic urges to denigrate the land to the west, to regard it as inferior and degenerate and threatening, in spite of all the evidence to the contrary. Our anti-Americanism is programmed into us. Cornelius de Pauw lives on. We still suspect that the American dog cannot bark.

And yet we are also in love. Anti-Americanism is not a simple phenomenon, a straightforward reaction to abuses, real or imagined. It is psychologically complex. Sometimes it coexists with strong feelings of attraction, sometimes even *because of* those feelings. What am I talking about? A visit to the Middle East and Latin America reveals the complexity of the relationship between reasonable people and the nation that seeks to impress, cajole, and – most importantly – to seduce them.

3. Egypt and Venezuela:
The view from the street

We might, not without some justification, compare
American culture to the AIDS virus, HIV.
> Margaret Wertheim, quoted in
> *Why Do People Hate America?*

ACTUALLY WE MIGHT not. At least not without leaving ourselves open to accusations of mind-numbing insensitivity to
suffering, coupled with an irrational loathing of happy end-
ings in films, or fizzy drinks, or hamburgers. What is fascinating about real hard-core, top-shelf anti-Americanism, is
that it really has limited appeal. It is exaggerated by those
within the US who use it for their own political ends (step
forward Fox News et al) and by those abroad who espouse
it so vehemently and, it has to be said, with such compelling
passion, that there is a tendency to believe they represent *the
true voice of the world.*

This is not to deny that the people of – for instance – the
Middle East or Latin America have a jaundiced view of the

USA. But in the post-Bush world, the popular foreign view of America, not just the way the nation is seen from afar but the way it is touched and tasted and smelled at home in smaller, less powerful nations around the globe, is complex and capable of change.

Before our brief visits to Cairo and Caracas I suppose we should take just a moment to state, and accept, the blindingly obvious. Obama's America still runs the world.

A simple train journey from New York to Washington brought it home to me soon after my arrival in the US. The trip is a three-hour canter through the post-industrial wastes of New Jersey, Pennsylvania and Maryland. The views are mostly gloomy; the train is slow; the bar has run out of beer. We could almost be in Britain. We lurch into Washington slightly late and the train conductor makes the usual announcements, and then, this: "Ladies and Gentlemen welcome to America's capital city, the capital city of *the free world*…"

They do not say that in Moscow or Beijing or London. Even at the height of Britain's imperial reach nobody suggested that freedom emanated from Waterloo Station. Never before has a fully democratic nation – publicly and self-consciously committed to freedom and universal human rights – been in such a position of power. And we are not talking here about military power. The extent of America's domination is much deeper, much more enduring, than that which could be enforced at the point of a gun.

American *cultural* hegemony is unparalleled in human

history. No one – expect perhaps a North Korean hermit – can avoid the tentacles of the American Dream. No one could avoid Obamamania. But the dream is not being foisted on the unwilling. In fact, the key to understanding its domination is to be found in the willingness of human beings around the globe to partake of it, or at least of parts of it. Zbigniew Brzezinski, once Jimmy Carter's National Security Advisor, puts it succinctly:

America has become the unplanned and politically unguided vehicle for a cultural seduction that seeps in, pervades, absorbs, and reshapes the external behaviour, and eventually the inner life, of a growing portion of mankind.

Brzezinski does not apologise for American pre-eminence but he does try to understand why it might be a little galling for the rest of us. That paragraph comes from *The Choice*, Brzezinski's warning to America that its power must be used wisely or eventually lost. Later in the book, he quotes Joseph Joffe, the German commentator on US affairs, making what I think is the most profoundly important point of all, if the nature of the relationship between America and the outside world is to be truly understood. Joffe says, "Seduction is worse than imposition. It makes you feel weak, and so you hate the soft-pawed corrupter, as well as yourself."

Aha. He is on to something.

Let us go on the briefest of world tours, an American-style, fast-paced trip to two capital cities, both of them in the heart of regions where the reality of American power has been much in evidence in recent decades, and has been much resented. Regions in which the soft-pawed corrupter has been busy...

> For sixty years my country, the United States, pursued stability at the expense of democracy in this region here in the Middle East and we achieved neither. Now we are taking a difference course. We are supporting the democratic aspirations of ALL people...

Well, what could be wrong with that? Condoleezza Rice was speaking in Cairo in 2006 at the American University: and as usual with Dr Rice, she was bang on message; the Bush second term had begun a year earlier with a ringing endorsement from the President of the business of making the world safe for democracy and democrats. Where better to start than with the tired old autocrats of the Middle East?

To many in the region, that speech came woefully late, and it came woefully unsupported by punchy action to ram the message home. As with previous American attempts to draw democratic lines in Middle Eastern sands, it floundered. Fully 50 years before the Rice speech, President Eisenhower appeared to be close to making a similar compact with the peoples of the area when, disregarding the squeals from London and Paris, he sided against the old colonial powers during the Suez crisis; sided against Israel as well. It looked to some in the region as if America really was setting out to become a serious long-term partner for moderate Arab nationalists. But the Cold War intervened and the Six Day War between Israel and its Arab neighbours. America ended up siding with Israel and a handful of Arab despots. This is the situation Dr Rice was addressing, and condemning to history.

One man took the message to heart. Ayman Noor was a liberal secular politician, who wanted to challenge President Hosni Mubarak. He decided to contest the 2006 elections. He decided to take America at its word.

According to the official figures, he received seven per cent of the vote. He has been in prison ever since, on trumped up charges of election fraud. Dr Rice has left the scene, as has President Bush; the promises they made, the promise of America, has been unfulfilled. Egypt, the Egypt of President Mubarak, continues to be the biggest recipient of US aid in the world after Israel. Complaints have been filed but nothing has been done.

America has a case to answer in the Middle East; a case that Washington is hypocritical, to put it mildly. This is a much wider point and a more interesting and substantial one than simply that the Bush administration made a mess of things. It is the case that America is mendacious, that the New World has spawned an arrogant power whose protestations about universal values and beacons of light are consciously empty.

In Cairo, they still do smoke-filled rooms. In the centre

of the city, I find myself in one, barely able to breathe, while a group of maybe 40 men prepare for a political meeting. I leave the room for some fresh air – standing outside at the top of an ornate colonial-era staircase, now grey and dusty and broken like so much of the city. There is a commotion in the room and suddenly the men are leaving; there is no panic, no sudden movement, but they are all heading past me and down the staircase. I stop one: What is happening? "There is a problem." What problem? "A problem." What problem? "I cannot tell you ..." And with that they are gone; leaving me almost alone with a middle-aged woman sitting calmly in a side room, her political meeting postponed, again. Gameela Ismail is the wife of Ayman Noor, the man who ran for president and ended up in jail. She runs the party now, though the task is extraordinarily difficult. Every day is, she says, "a small war". She tells me the supporters – mostly students – left in a hurry after hearing a rumour that the police were going to come and take the names of those attending. Democracy this is not.

So here is a real, live Middle Eastern woman who has been let down by America. And not just a little: her husband is in prison as a direct result of taking the Bush administration at its word. Her life is ghastly, she is harassed daily, she tells me with "all the kinds of threats that can face a woman in the Middle East in an Islamic culture." Surely there is no better proof of the emptiness, the shallowness, of the promise of America?

In fact, no. Gameela does not absolve President Bush. She is pointed: her husband, she says, is trapped in prison, the victim of his confidence in something that never really materialised. The Egyptian regime and the Bush administration are playing a game. But, she adds, she still has hope. "America is a dream. It is a destination for everyone who wants to go and live in a free and democratic place."

America is a dream. Even to those it lets down.

Across Cairo, another calmly authoritative woman agrees, "I think America is a force for good." The speaker is Hala Mustapha, a newspaper columnist and academic who introduced Dr Rice when she gave her speech in 2006. She is a member of the ruling party but a maverick, again under great pressure from the street, and from the police who pay her visits, and not because they want to know how she is. Hala Mustapha thinks she is still operating as a journalist because Dr Rice took a personal interest in her future, but the fact is that Dr Mustapha and Gameela Ismail have both been let down. And yet they aren't making plans to appeal for help from China or Russia or the European Commission. They know where help should be located: they know where they think help might one day lie. These women are not the voices of the street. You would not find them burning Danish flags after the Mohammed cartoons kerfuffle. I make no claim that they are representative of a putative Middle East wide, US appreciation society that has been overlooked by commentators in the past. But they are real flesh-and-blood liberal democrats, secular democrats of the kind the West is desperate to encourage and assist. And although both have been let down, both are sticking with America.

These "victims" of American seduction are disappointed, but not bitter.

Others respond less gently. "We have had almost 6000 years without the Americans in Egypt. I think we did pretty well!" This from a drama professor Mahmoud el Lozy, who puts the case against the United States with a vehemence that borders on self-parody. Mr Lozy is a difficult beast for Americans to pin down: he is not a religious zealot, not a "hater" of the kind so often decried during the 2008 election. It is not that he hates freedom: he just flatly denies that America loves it. It would not be possible to bomb Mr Lozy into submission, nor frighten him, nor charm him. Somehow America has to live with this: "Americans for some reason feel that they should be loved," he tells me with heavy sarcasm, "and if you don't love them then they are going to kill more of you until you do love them. They are going to beat you to a pulp until you love them. To me, this is the only kind of American exceptionalism I can think of."

I try: how about America's role of bringing freedom to those who do not have it? What about Eastern Europe, what indeed about Western Europe after the Second World War?

"America has waged possibly as many wars as most of humanity in a period of 2000 years, and all in the name of Freedom. Even Hitler didn't do that"

Some folks just aren't up for the message. America has to

swallow this. But this neuralgia has a cause and it goes back to Joseph Joffe and the "soft-pawed corrupter". Mr Lozy is a charming man, a humane man, with posters of Bob Dylan staring down from his study walls; he is not a mass killer or a potential mass killer. Yet America cannot get through to him: not with the exercise of old-fashioned "hard power", the kind that wins wars, nor with new-fangled "soft power" that fosters understanding and so eases the way – the thinking goes – for American interests to be fulfilled. When I suggest that Mr Lozy's issues are in his mind, I do not mean that in a patronising, pejorative way; this is an issue of psychology, not psychiatry, but either way, it is mental.

Oddly, the anti-American I met in Cairo with whom America could perhaps do the best business in the future was the one man no American diplomat would be allowed to meet at the moment, even under Obama's administration. He is a diminutive, wiry, tough, giggly fellow called Essam el Erian. He is a clinical pathologist at the medical centre in downtown Cairo, fresh out of prison after a five-year term for being a member of the semi-banned Moslem Brotherhood. Mr Erian is an anti-American too, but he allows that the *idea* of America is not necessarily a bad one. I asked him if he had any respect for America's core values and his reply seemed almost conciliatory: "I think, yes, they built in a few years a good state according to some important values. If they are searching for respect – respect OK – but why love?" Mr Erian, bird-like in his movements and demeanour, suddenly throws back his head and roars with laughter at the foolishness of the sad cases back in the USA, who search for love with such self-demeaning determination.

Both Mr Erian and Mr Lozy are amused by America's desire to be loved. They see it as pathology, a behavioural trait that sets the United States apart, and not in a good way. But this, I think, is a misunderstanding. America's desire to be loved is not the skin-deep touchiness that the Cairo anti-Americans perceive. This is a desire that speaks not of adolescent petulance but of a genuine American hunger to be judged differently, by both its own people and by foreigners, to be judged more harshly. American legitimacy rests on the "buy-in" of the rest of the world. Without the buy-in, it is hard to see what right America has to do what it does around the globe, what core legitimacy it can muster. But it is difficult to get there if the rest of the world is touchy about this seduction.

Talking of being touchy, let us leave Cairo and head west to Caracas:

> The Devil is right at Home. The Devil. The Devil himself is right in the house. And the Devil came here yesterday… Yesterday, ladies and gentlemen, from this rostrum, the President of the United States, the gentleman I refer to as the Devil, came here, talking as if he owned the world. Truly as the owner of the world.
>
> > Hugo Chavez, Venezuelan leader,
> > speaking at the United Nations.

Hugo Chavez is best known to British people as the political friend of Ken Livingstone who provided money for London buses. But to the Bush White House he was a constant source of irritation. Mr Livingstone was not the issue; Chavez was cosy with Iran. He was a supporter of Fidel Castro. He upset the US TV evangelist Pat Robertson so badly that the deranged preacher appeared to call – embarrassingly – for Mr Chavez to be assassinated. Chavez is a big figure whose influence extends throughout South America and whose presence is felt even in the North. He struts his stuff only a couple of hours from the southern border of the US; and does so well protected by a thick coating of oil. Venezuela is rich in oil reserves and its leader uses those reserves to bolster his regional power and fuel his regional voice, though with oil prices lower, so is the volume of his voice. Mr Chavez is part democrat, properly elected to office in a part of the world where that kind of thing is not always considered necessary; part would-be autocrat keen to solidify his hold on power beyond mere constitutional constraints; part serious man and part clown. Is he anti-American? He was certainly an enemy of President Bush, and his most ardent supporters are enemies of what they see as American imperialism in their region; an imperialism that stands as proof of the mendacity at the core of America's promise to the world.

It all started in 1823 with President Monroe and his Doctrine in which he set out for the world to see and refer back to centuries later, that the United States was not going to allow the Old World to meddle in its backyard. The Americas belonged to those who lived there, or would do in the future. The Europeans broadly took the message and stayed away, but Washington showed no such self-restraint, over the years launching more than 50 military interventions in South American nations, several aimed at democratic governments.

But there is more to it than that. To see the role of the US in South America merely in terms of coups and economic imperialism is to fall into an anti-American intellectual trap. Could it be that some of the anti-American feeling in these parts is a rather convenient smokescreen in countries where local people have had opportunities to thrive politically, socially, economically, but have not always grasped them?

I visited Caracas, the car-choked capital of Venezuela, where petrol is cheaper than bottled water. In the elegant lobby of a downtown hotel I met Augusto Montiel, a Birmingham University-educated enemy of American world domination: "The United States," he starts out, "has become culturally, sociologically, politically, economically, an empire. There is a culture in the United States about being the roof of the world."

But what of the positive things? I ask. What about the huge amount of fair trade with the United States, a trade that benefits people in their daily lives. America's motives surely are no different to those of other nations...

"Oh My God!" And he is off, talking about economies

laid waste by American policies, of the attacks on local sovereignty, of the IMF, the World Bank etc etc. "The United States has shaped the others to accept everything they say... That, my friend, is not free trade. That, my friend, is not democracy. That is dictatorship!"

But there is another view in Venezuela. Typically you hear it from the smooth-talking, whiskey-drinking elite, the cosmopolitan Latin movers and shakers who glide effortlessly, assisted often by a large number of passports, from one glitzy hotel to the next. They speak of American efforts to pull the levers of power in these parts as being desperately exaggerated. Antonio Herrera Vaillant is a business leader, stylishly dressed for our meeting in shocking yellow cords, and expensive loafers, the picture of moneyed confidence, and the picture too of pained disappointment at the lack of influence from the North. "There is a delusion that the United States is all powerful when it happens to be impotent most of the time," he tells me. "I have considered for years that the CIA is one of the most bumbling bureaucracies on the planet..." Mr Vaillant is criticising America for sure, but not for its over-indulgence in Latin meddling, in fact, for quite the opposite. Tapping into another rich seam of historical anti-American thought, Mr Vaillant sees the northerners, or at least their leaders, as imbeciles, simpletons, dangerously at sea in the real world.

The other fact of Latin American life is that anti-Americanism is tinged, deeply tinged, with a kind of grudging respect for the things that America can provide. Here, even more than in Cairo, the soft-pawed seducer has been at work and the seduction has spawned a rich array of emotions, running the whole gamut from hate to love and back again. You can spend a surprisingly moving evening at a McDonald's in Caracas: moving because you see Latin-American lower-middle-class strivers at play – their children rewarded with a trip to their favourite restaurant, their hard work paying off. José Bové – the French anti-McDonald's campaigner, would be sick at the sight of it; but McDonald's in Caracas does not smell to me of imperialism, cultural or culinary; it smells to me like freedom. Are people resentful at the dominance of the American chain? Perhaps they are. Perhaps some feel a kind of subliminal humiliation at the wide-eyed wonderment their children feel for Ronald McDonald. Perhaps some of them hate themselves for succumbing to the seducer's ever-easy charm.

But in a few years' time, I am sure that there will be a resurgence of interest in wholewheat tamale bars or whatever the local competition turns out to be, and McDonald's will be less fashionable as a family night out. I suspect that this is a phase, not a destination. And millions of Latin Americans benefit daily from the powerhouse of the US economy, from the things they can buy at home and from the money they receive from relatives cleaning cars in Los Angeles, making beds in Las Vegas, picking fruit in rural Georgia. This money is being sent from a healthy economy to many sick ones, where economic development is stymied by corruption. The US has behaved badly in South

America, and done it repeatedly, but to many South American families, it is still a lifeline.

So here is a legitimate question you do not often hear asked in Caracas: could the locals be at least partly to blame for local problems, local failings and local misery? In Latin America, whose population is roughly 500 million, 200 million live on less than two dollars a day. Why? Is it all the fault of the imperialists to the north? Or could just a little of it be linked to local attitudes, to honesty in government and the rule of law? In other words, is modern-day Latin anti-Americanism mainly an effort to hide the reality of local failure? "If something isn't working," says Otto Reich, "blame the Americans."

Mr Reich is the former US ambassador to Venezuela, born in Cuba and burning with that hatred of the Latin left that so many of his compatriots share. Mr Reich is not a gentle figure; some believe he was complicit in a coup attempt against Hugo Chavez. He denies it, but on the subject of anti-Americanism he is admirably open and blunt:

When you scratch the surface of some of these anti-Americans you find self-loathing people, a lot of them. They despise the fact that their countries grew up, emerged into the world at the same time as the United States with very similar ideals... And yet they have not been able to progress. Why? Because of a culture that has enabled corruption, inefficiency, and unwillingness to innovate... The people are the same; they have the same number of bones, the same number of cells in their brains. Why don't they progress? It's because they are not brought up with the same values ...

Easy now. The Spanish word *prepotente* (arrogance) is often used to describe this North American approach and as I listen to Otto Reich, I must admit I begin to feel quite sorry for the losers in the South. This talk of values is important and salutary but it cannot hide the dangerous "values" of American fruit-picking companies down the years, who have seen South America as their backyard and not one they needed to keep pretty.

Each side needs to own up to getting the relationship wrong, it seems to me: Washington first, as the place where the Monroe Doctrine was first promulgated, and where the invasions into Latin America were conceived and the commercial domination approved and facilitated. But then the South too, because the Southerners, in their heart of hearts, know the reason why Otto Reich's words hurt so badly is that they are just the teeniest bit true.

My journeys to Cairo and Caracas were not intended to reveal scientific truths about anti-Americanism. But it is an interesting fact that some of those whom the United States could be said to have let down, still love America and depend on its promise. Others, who have been left alone, fume in more or less sullen hatred. Still more are willing to give grudging respect to the Great Satan, if only it would leave them alone. Some anti-Americans, the most dangerous kind in terms of their ability to harm individual human beings, I have deliberately left out of this chapter; they are not driven by the same demons as the wider anti-US crowd. But talking to anti-Americans brings home the need that America has to explain itself to a world that likes the taste of American stuff but, sated, feels sick and looks for someone to blame. Or, to stick with the seduction metaphor, has woken up the next day with a headache and a sense of shame. But the seducer is really not so bad; America is troubled, to be sure, but it is worth getting to know.

4. Does America Exist?

IN THE CLASSIC cowboy series *The Virginian*, we never learned the true name of the eponymous hero. Let us be daring and presume that he came from the state of Virginia. The story is based in Wyoming, in the west, so he is far from home, but little more about his background is revealed. He is white, of course; he is also silent and strong. When someone needs hanging, he hangs them.

What if a modern-day Virginian were to arrive in Wyoming and take part in a modern-day version of the films? What would a modern-day Virginian look like?

George Allen, a Republican politician once regarded as a future president, thought of himself as the epitome of the modern-day Virginian. Until 2006, he represented Virginia in the Senate. He was the son of a famous American football coach. He was gruff and rugged and plain-spoken, and, like the TV Virginian, a believer in tough love and tough justice. In his law firm office, he had a noose hanging from a tree.

In the 2006 mid-term elections, Allen met with a disaster. He had been followed round during the campaign by a man working for his Democratic opponent. The man, of Indian descent, had been videotaping his meetings and generally making the Virginian feel uncomfortable. On August 11th, during a stop in a small town near the Virginia-Kentucky border, Senator Allen broke. The words he uttered destroyed his career: "So, welcome, let's give a welcome to Macaca here! Welcome to America and the real world of Virginia!" "Macaca" is a racially derogative term hailing from the French colonies. Goodness knows why the Virginian chose to use it. But use it he did. And he went on to lose the election and his entire political career.

And here is the twist. S. R. Sidarth, the man Senator Allen accused – by implication at least – of being some racially inferior foreigner taking advantage of the wonders of American freedom, turned out to be as American as, well, George Allen. In fact, he was a fellow Virginian. Howard Fineman, the *Newsweek* columnist, reveals in his book, *13 American Arguments*, that Sid, as Sidarth was known to his friends, was one of the finest products of the prosperous Indian American community who make up an important element of northern Virginian life. Sid was an academic and athletic star. He was also a Democrat, a supporter of a party that has campaigned at least intermittently for gay rights and gun control. Sid was no cowboy. And yet according to the online magazine *Slate*: "He, not Allen, was the true Virginian."

Who, then, are the Americans that the haters hate? What do they look like? Where do they come from? These questions are hardly ever asked by the anti-American crowd and with good reason. They want us to see only their caricature of Uncle Sam. This caricature is almost always a white man. He is sometimes a cowboy, violent and unsophisticated, the Virginian of old; and if not a cowboy, he is a couch potato, fat and ignorant and ill-informed about the outside world; at best both of these characters are naïve, at worst downright nasty. Representative Americans, according to this caricature, are ugly Americans. Exceptions exist: Bob Dylan, Martin Luther King, Virginian Sid and now Barack Obama. But the idea persists, the idea is encouraged to persist, of an ugly entity: "an American". Friendly Americans – who write jazz or lead reform movements or inspire international respect in some other field – are something different; belonging to "another America" which is somehow placed (geographically, it sometime seems) away from the "real" place.

True enough, there are plenty of fat, white people in America slurping double grande Pepsis in heartland shopping malls. Some of them are very nice people as well; kindly people not given to issuing *fatwas* or starting wars. Some came to Sarah Palin rallies during the 2008 election and wondered if Barack Obama was an *A-rab,* it is true, but generally these folk are harmless. But here is my point: they are not where the action is in this nation; they are not the future. To concentrate on them is to ignore the other corners of the US where just as many people live, and to ignore the direction America is taking. Younger people, better-educated people, the people of the future, do not live in Kansas. Barack's mum left the place for a reason.

Here's a better place to find the future: San Antonio, Texas. Most anti-Americans (most foreigners) would have trouble placing San Antonio on a map though it is one of the biggest cities in the United States. Founded by the Spanish in the seventeenth century, it is home to the Alamo and some striking Spanish-style architecture – sections of the city have the look of Cordoba or the old parts of Malaga. The Spanish, of course, are long gone. But Spanish speakers are everywhere here; immigrants from Spain's South American empire live among some of the earliest remnants of that empire. San Antonio is home to an overwhelmingly Latino population. More than 60 per cent of San Antonians identify themselves as Latino. I walked around the city centre with an American friend who was brought up in San Francisco but whose family, like Virginian Sid's, came from India. The Tex-Mex culture of San Antonio – shops selling stetsons and cowboy boots, the physical look of so many of the people, the whole ambience – was a shock to Aditya, my Indian American friend. He speaks no Spanish and would look decidedly odd in cowboy boots. He had no idea that San Antonio was so exotic. Yet behind his surprise was a kind of pride that such a discovery might be waiting for him in his own land. Both Aditya and the people of San Antonio are fully American and when the outside world complains about Americans, these are the folk they should have in mind – cowpunchers from San Antonio who are half-Mexican in outlook – and intellectual nervy chaps with family in Delhi. This is the nation.

But before meeting more of them, we have to establish some kind of agreement that America itself exists, that "The United States" is a place we can all recognise and describe in a way that can be approved of by reasonable people. The Declaration of Independence, interestingly, does not mention the nation, speaking instead of "Free and Independent States". The idea of nationhood, in other words, was not at the core of the enterprise on day one. Freedom came first. Decentralisation was the founding aim. Americans have never had a debate about devolution, that ghastly bureaucratic term that describes Britain's halting – and not much appreciated – steps towards local control of local affairs. In the US, from the start it was perfectly obvious that power should be exercised locally. It still is. Freedom for communities was more prized than nationhood. As one of America's first congressmen Fisher Ames put it in 1792, "Instead of feeling as a nation, a State is our Country."

Later on, when the issue of secession arose, with the slaveholding states wanting to go their own way, the northern army that defeated them was not the "National" army, it was the "Union" army. Union of what was never definitively answered. Only after the Civil War, and partly at least as a reaction to this terrible slaughter and the desire that it be worthwhile in the longer term, was American nationalism born and encouraged. In the century after the war, it took flight as an idea – attachment to locality is still a feature of American life, and a rather wonderful one, but attachment to the nation obviously exists as well – and the federal government (more properly described as the national government) in Washington is plainly now of pre-eminent importance in American public life. Yet not in private lives. And the relationship between local attachment and national attachment is complex.

Watching Barack Obama in early 2008 working a crowd in Ohio, I noticed that he understood that localism needed to have its limits: he thanked the local crowd (it was in a place called Dayton, which, typically, had its own local bomb squad with their own bomb squad vehicle proudly standing outside the venue) and then got carried away with a rendition of the local teams – basketball, football etc, and their team mottos, Go, Turtles! or Attaboy Chubbies! (I am making the details up) – until the roars of appreciation began to morph into competition between the various subgroups. Yikes! Enough, the candidate cried. Before the Turtles attacked the Chubbies and all hell broke loose, Hello Dayton and hello Ohio. Hello America.

You see it in every corner of the nation, this commitment to something small and local, and at the same time a commitment every bit as strong to something much larger. *E pluribus unum*.

There is a mountain path outside Missoula in the

foothills of some of Montana's most fabulous mountain scenery. Halfway up the path there are two signs, each quintessentially American. The first reads: "No trespassing, *survivors* will be prosecuted!" The second, scrawled on a Stars and Stripes: "God Bless America". There is a commitment here to a vigorous defence of private property, an attachment to a locality and privacy. But there is also a commitment, every bit as strong, to the wider nation, to the *whole* of America.

America's greatest achievement is also the cause of the greatest resentment among modern Europeans: Americans care. They are attached – to their guns and the right to use them, but more importantly to families, to communities, and of course, most famously to their nation. They fly flags. They believe: in themselves, in God, *in stuff*. They are proud of their identities. While Europeans fret about their colonial past and wonder whether they have the right to impose cultural choices on others, Americans fight for what they believe in. Some acquaintances of mine in Washington begin their rather grand dinner parties with grace; there is a pause for effect and then the mother offers a toast: "Death to al-Qaeda!" To world-weary Europeans this attachment to identity, this willingness to put up fists to defend it, can seem naïve at best, infantile and myopic at worst. But it gives American society a unique strength – a strength that comes from the constant knowledge that you love your family, your community, your town, your university, your church, your nation, your culture. You are allowed to feel unique. You are the best! And so is your nation.

In Europe we are not sure that we are the best. Perhaps our gloom is justified. But to American eyes, we can seem mighty weak; colourless and valueless, drifting rather than living. Americans have a zest for life. When things go well for them, they have no trouble believing that they deserve it.

But never forget that America is a slightly vacuous concept. Keep in mind that the idea of nationhood was an invention after the fact. America was not created by men who wanted to build a united homogenous country. This coloured and continues to colour the American experience. It is one of the reasons why black people suffered in the south long after the rest of the nation had decided such suffering was a "national" embarrassment, and it accounts as well for the peculiar voting practices – locally born and nurtured with huge local pride – that so bemused and fascinated the outside world as the 2008 election got under way. It accounts for the richness and the variegation of the American experience.

But rich and variegated as it is, you cannot seriously argue these days that America – an entity you can describe as a unified structure with common aims and a roughly unified world view – does not exist. No Montanan thinks of himself as anything but an American. These United States – as the founding fathers called them – have become one.

What then of the people who inhabit this place? My Indian American friend and the folks down in San Antonio are all fairly recent immigrants – though actually, by modern standards, Aditya is *Mayflower*-esque in his US longevity; he was born here. That is the first fact to get straight: that by 2025, according to the well-respected experts at the Pew Research Center, an extraordinary fifteen per cent of US citizens will have been foreign-born. And yet America is not – as is so often and so lazily suggested – a nation of immigrants. It is a nation of settlers. This nation is more than an agglomeration of humanity.

Nor does that description entirely grasp it; the US is a nation of settlers with attitude. It is true that Aditya is culturally separate from his fellow Americans in southern Texas. And yet, and here is the genius of the place, they are bound by ties both sides would acknowledge as hugely important – going to the heart of who they are.

Take a different and imaginary example; an aging hippie living in San Francisco and an oil mogul living in Houston do not, on the face of it, have much in common. The hippie might have wanted to vote for Dennis Kucinich in the 2008 election (he's the left-wing Democrat from Ohio, with a wife who hails from Upminster and has a pierced tongue) and the oil man for Ron Paul (the libertarian Republican who wanted to abolish income tax and close down public education) but they probably both compromised – for the respective Republican and Democratic nominees – and they probably both accept the other's right to win. At a deeper cultural level, the two grew up with, react against, or cleave towards the same cultural underpinnings – the puritan past, the geofreedom, the sense of America's promise, even if they disagree about whether, or how, that promise can be fulfilled. They recognise each other. But they do not recognise each other in the same way as other nationalities do. A poll taken after the Obama victory (but before the inauguration) suggested that large numbers of Republicans embraced him in more than a grudging "I respect the system" terms: they were actually optimistic about the nation! Nowhere else in the western world would this be the case. Americans cannot help thinking positively about what is to come. American coexistence, American society, is based not on shared blood or world experience, but on the promise of a shared future – "We live," as the commentator David Brooks has put it, "in the future tense."

"We are not an imaginative people," he writes, "a dreaming people. Middle Americans may not be contemplative or dark and brooding. We may not be rooted in a deep and mysterious past. But we do have our heads in a vast and complicated future."

My daughter Clara is part of that future. She is half-American. No, that's wrong; you cannot be half-American. Clara is 100 per cent American. Clara's mum and dad are British through and through, and Clara has a British passport. But by accident of birth (we were already living in Washington when she was born) she leaves us behind. To get her British passport, there were hoops to be jumped through, stipulations to be noted, and requirements to be fulfilled. For the US passport there were none. She *is* American because she was born here. Her parents do not matter, nor does her colour or creed, her ancestry, or the cut of her jib. She is a natural-born citizen, to use the rubric of the constitution, and provided she lives in the US for a bit and pays her taxes and achieves the age of 35, she can be president. She is as American as any other of her 300 million fellow citizens.

This fact staggers me. Much fuss has been made of Barack Obama's heritage. But putting him to one side, America gets precious little praise for the simple moral force of its open source composition. America is not open in a passive kind of a way – the nation has sought out immigrants over the years and seeks them out still. Openness is a part of the American Creed.

But hold on, the sceptics cry. Are there not Americans who want to end the "birthright citizenship" that gave Clara her start towards the presidency? True, there are: a group of seventeen Republicans introduced a bill in Congress in 2005 to do just that. And this commitment to openness – this openness myth – has not always been entirely honoured. The anti-birthright bill got nowhere but what about the internment of Japanese Americans in World War II? What about the racially charged exclusion of Jews from polite society here, and of Italians or Irish Americans when those groups first set foot on US soil? Is it not a fact that Chinese people were banned from coming to America – the Chinese Exclusion act was America's first full-scale effort to cut down on immigration. Back in 1882, these unfortunates were condemned by the Supreme Court as a "menace to our civilisation", just four years before the Statue of Liberty was raised in New York harbour. Above all, is it not a fact that hostility to the recent influx of Mexicans – legal and illegal – has exposed once again this tendency of Americans to talk the talk on openness but not, when it comes to it, to walk the walk? In fact, that same phrase – "a menace to our civilisation" – is used now to describe the Mexicans and their perceived inability to assimilate into mainstream US culture.

It is certainly true that illegal immigration and the threat (as many see it) of bilingualism is a big deal in the modern US. In a church in Wichita, Kansas (the congregation looking very much like the Americans of that stereotype, white and podgy, their children sour-looking and primly dressed), the preacher told me it was the biggest issue of all in his area. Speaking in the run-up to the 2008 election, before the Republicans had even chosen their candidate, he confidently predicted that the prize would go to the Republicans because they alone could deal with the illegals. I think he had in mind a Biblical flood, with legal citizens in arks and everyone else drowned. I am serious; this was Wichita.

But what happened? Well, on the Republican side, the party chose (in John McCain) the one candidate who was solidly and totally behind the idea of giving legal status to illegal immigrants. They rejected nativism. Even with twelve million illegal immigrants in the US, even with Spanish spoken increasingly often in large swathes of the nation, even though recession was looming and personal wealth (in the form of housing) reducing, they still chose John McCain.

In fact, one of the central features of the 2008 election was the collapse, the ignominious defeat, of the nativist tendency in the Republican Party. Tom Tancredo, the anti-illegal immigration candidate for the presidency, got nowhere. Tancredo, who has called for a moratorium on legal immigration as well, and who once referred to Miami as a third-world city on account of its large Latino population, was run out of town like a no-good foreigner. Mitt Romney, the clean-cut Mormon who once championed undocumented workers' rights, took up the cudgels on behalf of Tancredo after he dropped out but got thoroughly burned for his efforts. Once asked to focus on the practicalities of how to transport twelve million illegal immigrants back to South America – on buses? – the natural moderation of Americans kicked in. The question was posed, gently but firmly, by those sympathetic to the plight of the modern-day huddled masses, and it was never really answered because the answer (make life so unpleasant for these people that they *beg* to go home) was a political non-starter. John McCain had clashed the most with the anti-illegal crowd. True enough, there is still a huge tension over illegal immigration – and true enough, that tension has always existed. But America is not a natural home of exclusion, racial or economic. In his Christmas message in 1982, Ronald Reagan – no bleeding-heart liberal – summed up the American way when he quoted from a letter sent home from a US sailor serving somewhere in the pacific:

> I know we're crowded and we have unemployment and we have a real burden with refugees, but I honestly hope and pray we can always find room. We have a unique society, made up of cast-offs of all the world's wars and oppressions, and yet we're strong and free. We have one thing in common – no matter where our forefathers came from, we believe in that freedom. I hope we always have room for one more person, maybe an Afghan or a Pole or someone else looking for a place... where he doesn't have to worry about his family's starving or a knock on the door in the night.

Of course, one reason (alright, the main reason) the Republicans turned against nativism is self-interest, and this itself tells you something about what modern America is and about who modern Americans are. Latinos make up huge proportions of some states. In time they will intermarry and interbreed. They vote. Many of their views on social issues such as abortion are much closer to the Republican Party than the Democrats. They are a constituency to be courted.

And courted they will be; by the Republicans, by the Democrats, but at a deeper level, a more interesting level, by the nation itself. By the American Creed.

The Creed is the ground zero of what the United States is about. It is "life, liberty and the pursuit of happiness", but it is much more than that. Anyone who knows anything about America knows that Americans themselves seem to think of their land as special. You do not have to be French to find this annoying. Americans think their nation is unique. They think this unique place contains a message for the outside world. This trait – it's been described as American exceptionalism – is challenged by the anti-Americans who attack it from two standpoints; that the reality does not live up to the American dream, and that whether or not the dream matches the reality, *we do not need this dream, thank you very much!* The rest of the world, the thinking goes, has no need for the heavy-handed affection of *faux* Texan pillocks like George Bush lecturing it on any-thing from "strategery" to brush-clearing.

Oh but it does! And here is why…

The first point is that this failure of the creed to match up to the reality of life is not a weakness – it is a strength. America's creed does not describe a cosy status quo, with problems swept under the carpet and Stepford Wife subur-bia imposed on a brainwashed people. No, the point of the creed is that it challenges existing behaviour, existing condi-tions. It is a constant call to arms. Just as the Christian gospel is said by some to comfort the afflicted and afflict the comfortable, so America's creed performs this duel role: both soothing and roughing up.

Foreigners invented the term "the American Creed". G. K. Chesterton coined it, and the Swedish economist Gunnar Myrdal popularised it within the US, calling it "the cement in the structure of this great and disparate nation".

Was his description a piece of hagiography by a smitten tourist? Far from it. Myrdal was writing in the 1940s and concentrating in particular on race relations; in other words, he was well aware of the fact that the creed did not result instantly in the practical reality of its promise. But Myrdal said the creed would triumph in the end, such was the power invested in it; whites could not live for ever in this schizophrenic condition of espousing liberty while denying it to millions of their fellow citizens. It turns out he was right – look at Barack Obama – but also wrong, as I point out elsewhere, because the divide between blacks and all other races in the US is a fundamental faultline, still dangerous and still wide.

That is the point about the creed. It is an *aspiration* for life, liberty and the pursuit of happiness, often rather undermined by daily life. But a weaker creed would have died under the weight of these contradictions. This one – rather like the central truths in the works of Shakespeare, or indeed of Christianity – lives on from year to year, decade to decade, century to century. Why?

Because America's creed is *our* creed. Our human creed. It speaks directly to all of us. You can sneer at the idea of American equality of opportunity (there is, after all, some surprise that the next president is not a Clinton or a Bush) and you can disparage the notion that individuals count for more than society – does that not lead to private affluence and public squalor? – but what you cannot argue with is the simple fact that America, as well as being hated, is, well, popular. There is something about this idea of individual liberty, something about the notion of personal responsibility, something about equality of opportunity, that all human beings – left to their own devices – seem to find attractive. America is what happens when humans take their chances, seize the moment, go for it. The creed gives flight to this collective desire. And when individuals decide that some aspect of society does not live up to the promise of the creed – well, there is a rallying point for reform.

You could write an entire book about how the creed fails the reality test. Many have. But to do that misses the point. The creed of Americanism pushes at the doors of the possible; it is that "future-tense" thinking that David Brooks has identified as one of the central traits of his fellow countrymen. Forget the squalor of much of America; try to put out of your mind the endless hopeless vistas of filling stations and purveyors of cheap doughnuts. And above all, do not get hung up on materialism.

"Getting things" is undoubtedly a by-product of the creed, but if that was all there was to it, if Americanism was simply about wealth creation and hoarding *stuff,* the place would be moribund. Of course there have been Americans who have believed it is. This is the dismal picture painted with such humour by the brilliant novelist Kurt Vonnegut; the picture of an empty American core. He says of one of his characters, "Like so many Americans, she was trying to construct a life that made sense from things she found in gift shops."

Ouch. Gift shops are a feature of life in the United States. They are often deeply depressing. It's difficult to feel anything but contempt for the overweight, underinformed coach-tour passengers easing their vast frames into Indian reservation gift shops around Monument Valley, Arizona to buy useless, crappy trinkets designed by the remnants of the tribes who once ruled this place. Modern Americans – set against the backdrop of the sheer physical glory of this place – can seem deeply unimpressive. Surely their pre-eminence is some kind of sick joke. But the America that created them is also the America that recognised the genius of Kurt Vonnegut and many others who have criticised and changed American society.

As David Brooks puts it: "If Middle America is so stupid, vulgar, self-absorbed, and materialistic, which it often is, then how can America be so great?" The answer to this reasonable question is that the stupidity, the vulgarity, the self-absorption, the materialism, is all of it a by-product of something vital and strong and lean and nimble and clever at the heart of the project: it's the American talent for striving. Brooks calls it "a Utopian fire that redeems its people", but you don't have to reach for such grandiose language to define it; this Utopian fire is the striving for human betterment – material, yes, but mental, and moral as well – that creates the restlessness that is America.

It can be positively corny. Years ago I visited the chilly northern city of Minneapolis. I was there in September and it was already snowing. Many Minneapolans

(Minneapolitans, Minneapolitanos?) don't come from these parts. Their smooth, light-brown skin and skinny, angular features do not speak of generations of fur trapping on the Canadian border, generations of September snow. These people come from the great lakes, to be sure: Africa's great lakes, on the east of the continent, around Ethiopia, Eritrea and Somalia.

Many are Moslems, doubly out of place in a part of the world where the freezing, ice-filled wind attacks you from a near horizontal angle and the prevailing religion is Lutheran Christianity.

Now, don't get me wrong. I am sure plenty of east African inhabitants of Minneapolis are miserable. I am sure plenty wish life had turned out differently, and plenty notice that a culture based on moose fancying and wood carving is not one over which they feel any sense of ownership, particularly when money is too tight for the pleasures of Minneapolis life to be available to them.

But plonk them down in Europe, for instance in a tower block in the suburbs of Paris, and the chances are they stay miserable, and stay alienated, and their kids stay that way as well. Other societies would let them rot and fester and plot. Plonk them in Minneapolis and transformation is possible – a transformation which cuts both ways, providing hope for them and willing citizens for the nation.

I bump into Omar from Somalia who escaped from war and lives here now with his 27-year-old daughter. Omar speaks broken English but fluent Arabic; he gets his news from his satellite television tuned to Al Jazeera and Al Arabiya. So far, so multicultural.

Omar is not in any sense a typical American and the world view gleaned from those sources is hardly likely to engender a love of the Stars and Stripes. And yet Omar says he likes it here and is thankful for the opportunities given to him. In particular he takes pride in the success of his daughter (already a change is being wrought) who has been to college and is now a translator. She has, he says in a matter-of-fact way, not had time to get married yet.

Bingo. Americanisation has begun. If she does get married and have kids, they will eat Somali food but think American thoughts. And America will gain another generation of hopeful people, for whom life is an upward curve. Yes, there will be a materialistic side to this curve; yes, there is a risk that they will get fat and do nothing with their lives; but possibilities are being created, which, frankly, would not exist anywhere else on earth.

Here's another example from the other end of the country and from a completely different set of immigrants, about as different as it is possible to be. It's raining cats and dogs at the Casa Bacardi. I've parked under palm fronds from which water cascades in positively tropical torrents. Air-conditioning has cooled the inside of my hire car but when I open the door, the heat and the moisture shock the senses. This could be a Latin American scene – and in many ways it is. Yes, Miami is a US city – it has Starbucks and Dunkin' Donuts and gas stations and skyscrapers and roads,

roads, roads – but scratch the surface and you draw Latin blood. The airwaves crackle with the Spanish language. You can sit in a restaurant and be the only English speaker in earshot. They come from many countries, these exiles, and for many reasons, but my interest is in the dominant group – the Cubans, who came for one reason: Fidel Castro.

I walk into the Casa Bacardi, soaked by the hot rain. Inside the building a small group – perhaps twenty people – has gathered for a guitar recital. Casa Bacardi has been funded by the Bacardi family, heirs to the rum fortune. It's a self-styled Cuban cultural centre, though the culture it celebrates is very definitely the dance and music and politics of the old days. The scene tonight is very genteel – I look like something the cat dragged in but the others at this soirée look magnificent, the women perfumed and prinked, the men ultra-cool in expensive black T-shirts and designer suits. They show their tropical credentials by looking immaculate although they must have come through the same storm that I did – perhaps an innate sense of Cuban rhythm allowed them to dodge the drops.

These are young Cuban Americans or to put it more precisely, young American Cubans. Mum and Dad came here decades ago, and Mum and Dad pray every night for Castro to meet with a terrible accident – and were disappointed and sad when the Cuban leader finally gave up power at a time of his own choosing. But Mum and Dad have also prospered in business in Miami and passed on a fair bit of wealth to the new generation, and the new generation feels at home here – *is* at home here. They will go to the island one day but not to reclaim property or fight communist remnants – they will go, they say, as tourists. The guitarists strike up and all seems very harmonious, very peaceful, very laid-back. Time has not healed Cuba's scarred politics – that would be a miracle – and there is certainly every chance that Castro's demise will be accompanied by violence, but perhaps when the time comes, the old generation will have run out of fight – and the new generation will be interested in more than settling scores. The new generation, even of this prickly and resentful and cohesive group of immigrants – immigrants, let us not forget, who don't even want to be American, who did not choose to come here – this new generation has become American. Blood ties and blood feuds have faded in salience; success, prosperity, "future orientation" have set in. A fair number of them voted for Obama, and hope that vote will lead to a normalisation of relations between Havana and Washington.

There is an understanding in America that life is here to be shaken up and examined and rearranged and lived and ultimately to be *celebrated*.

That's the piece of the American Creed we ignore too often when we examine it from afar: *It's the pursuit of happiness, stupid!* Not bad for a national vocation. Not bad for a human vocation.

But why bother the rest of us with it? Why do Americans think it translates to the outside world? Is this not evidence of their desire to subjugate us all – the desire for American empire? No. America's vocation, in the words of David Frum, a right-of-centre intellectual, "is not an imperial vocation. It is a vocation to support justice with power".

"If a foreign people lack liberty, it is not through some misguided act of cultural choice. It is because they have been seized and oppressed and tyrannised. To say that we are engaged in 'imposing American values' when we liberate people, is to imply that there are people on earth who value their own subjugation."

Now Frum – a friend of mine – supported the Iraq war and still does. Worse: he used to write George Bush's speeches. He wrote those words on America's vocation while Bush was still in power.

So are they irrelevant now? I don't think so. Anyone looking to the next four or eight years as being years of repudiation of the essential message of America abroad is in for a disappointing time. There are disagreements about what constitutes "power" – and questions of degree when it comes to supporting justice – but America is not about to give up on its core belief, its capacity to do good around the world. During the Cold War, as many former cold warriors now openly accept, American often did the wrong thing, backed "our son of a bitch" in the hope of getting the right result in the long term. And at the end of the Cold War, there was a real wobble about what America would stand for, would do, in the future. As the novelist John Updike put it, "Without the Cold War, what's the point of being an American?"

Well, there is still a point. To spell it out, America stands (imperfectly, yes, but truly) for individual rights, for the belief that individuals always matter; that no human being genuinely opts for oppression, religious, political or cultural. The message of America is an in-your-face message and the knowledge that Americans think of themselves as superior can be a little annoying, but neither fact detracts from one tiny nugget of truth: that the message of America is the best message available. It beats the message of Moscow or Beijing or Tehran, or indeed Brussels. The world is already a pretty awful place for large numbers of our fellow citizens but a world without American power would be incalculably worse, for millions of Taiwanese people for instance, or Israelis, or for women in Afghanistan, for Kosovo Albanians, for sub-Saharan Africans benefiting from funds to combat AIDS, and in a wider sense, for all of us Europeans who know that if push comes to shove, the Yanks will bail us out, as they did our parents and theirs before them.

The Archbishop of Canterbury, Rowan Williams, criticised Americans in 2008 for being less-caring imperialists than even the British had been. He went further. The problem was wider than American imperialism: Western modernity itself "is eating away at the soul".

I like Western modernity. It allows my children to survive diseases that would have killed them only decades ago.

My son has juvenile diabetes; western modernity (insulin and medical intervention) keeps him alive. It also creates educational opportunities our ancestors never had; opportunities for leisure and fun and fulfilment. And it is protected, guaranteed around the world (to the extent that it is guaranteed at all) mainly by American power. It is not guaranteed by China or Russia or Tehran or Brussels. Yes, this modernity, particularly at its American extreme, also creates opportunities for type 2 diabetes (the type you can get from bad diet) and crushing *ennui*, and for the kind of queasy feelings from which the gentle Archbishop apparently suffers. But to focus on the downside of Western modernity is not to tell the whole story. People want it. And America provides it.

Of course, this American embrace is not always comfortable; sometimes it crushes those it should be saving, sometimes it carelessly ignores information or intelligence that would have helped its case; sometimes it allows itself to be hijacked by those whose aims are less honourable (remember the exiled Iraqi businessman and would-be politician Ahmed Chalabi who seduced the Bush crowd with what turned out to be an utterly unrealistic vision of how the invasion would play out); all of that is true. But the myth of America abroad is still a myth backed, at least intermittently, by solid evidence of real worthiness of purpose and real guts in delivering betterment around the world. Again: time to forget President Bush and look at the guts of the message, and the actual behaviour of America, at home and abroad. Ask Africans if America is a malign influence on their world (even President Bush was popular in many African nations); or survivors of the Asian tsunami or the Pakistan earthquake. Look too at the fights America has picked. They are fights in keeping with the message of the creed.

No other nation does this. Abroad, no other nation fights the fight out of such a sense of universal relevance and responsibility. And at home no other nation has a self-correcting national myth that informs and challenges and renews with such vigour, such gusto. America's creed makes it unique. If you are Scottish or Armenian or Pakistani or Thai or Chinese or Australian, you do not have it. If you hail from any of those places and you have taken US citizenship, you do.

"How weird is that?" as my children would say. And how wonderful.

5. Freedom

THE SIGNATURE PUDDING dish in the cafeteria of the Bush White House was called Chocolate Freedom. It had a chocolate base, an ice cream middle, and was topped with sparklers. It was quite a confection. They were proud of it, but I am not aware that the dish caught on elsewhere in the world; the parallel between the chocolate version of freedom and the policy version as cooked up by the White House is obvious: both were confections designed to appeal to American palates, neither had much of a sense of permanence about it, and too much of either appeared to make you sick.

In the past few years, America has promised much in the deliverance of freedom and achieved, well, not as much as it promised. Proof, the attackers cry, of malign intentions; of failure to defend freedoms at home and a weakness for global adventures, driven less by genuine belief in the freedom creed, and more by a desire to conquer and dominate.

I want to make the case that appearances are deceptive:

that Americans are about as naturally imperialistic as guinea pigs. American imperialism is not quite an oxymoron but it is close. They are not after us; they do not want to control us, at least not in a bad way. American freedom, America's attachment to the idea of individual liberty and imperfect but real practice of this faith, is the single most important factor in the prevention of American empire. In this sense, the Obama presidency is irrelevant: even if it looks prettier to foreign eyes, it does not change the fundamentals. The fundamentals are anti-imperial.

My son complains that America doesn't always look rich; it doesn't always look free either. A good friend was held up at gunpoint outside a metro station in suburban Maryland, just on the outskirts of Washington. "Give me your money," the gunman demanded. As my friend described it, that request was not difficult to comply with: "Take it," she said, "take everything, take the credit cards as well." But then – in spite of the fact that she was facing a clearly desperate man in very dangerous circumstances – she stopped the gunman before he fled and begged him to reconsider one item among those he was about to make off with. Please, she said, *please* do not take my Washington DC driving licence.

My friend risked her life to keep her driving licence because the alternative – trying to get a replacement from the DMV, the Department of Motor Vehicles – seemed at the time to be such a dreadful prospect that death itself might be less onerous.

Bureaucracy is shockingly inept and shockingly prevalent

in the self-proclaimed land of the free. The dead-eyed denizens of the DMV are peculiarly difficult to deal with: I have a letter in front of me informing me that an inspection, the local equivalent of an MOT, is due on my vehicle by a certain date; but the date is wrong. "Disregard the letter," an unsmiling employee advises me, but this is only to deal with the immediate problem that I am standing at her desk and she wants me to go away. It does not address the substance: that a computer will notice that I have not had my car inspected as it requires and will adjudge me to be what they call in these parts a "delinquent" and will fine me relentlessly, monthly, until I comply with the erroneous request. But if I do try to comply, the inspectors will not inspect because the date on the car sticker is too far in advance. The term Kafkaesque is overused, but Kafkaesque this undoubtedly is. And sadly, the DMV is not a rogue organisation. There is a strand of bureaucratic, paper-pushing, rule-bound small mindedness running through the guts of the United States; which is why food rotted while people went hungry in New Orleans after Hurricane Katrina. It may even be why Osama Bin Laden survived the pre-9/11 efforts to track him down and kill him; when they got him in the cross-hairs, the story goes, there was no one around in Washington with sufficient legal clearance to be able to say "shoot!"

Living in America means following rules. Our own arrival here, as bright-eyed seekers of freedom, fresh from a stint in bureaucratic and stifling Brussels, contained an early hint of the rigours to come; on the first few occasions that we drew in beside our new home in our oversized people carrier, we parked sometimes on the left side of the road and sometimes on the right. It depended from which direction we had driven into the street. We didn't care. Let Freedom Reign, we thought, or would have done if we had thought about parking at all. Until a neighbour came up the steps to the porch with a warning: you can be fined, she said, for doing that. 'That' turned out to be parking against the flow of traffic; in Brussels you can park in the middle of the road and nobody bats an eyelid. Pioneers in the New World allow no such licence.

But here is the great American paradox: annoying as many of these rules can be, the national obsession with law is wonderfully liberating as well. Respect for the constitution destroyed the efforts of some religious zealots to circumvent it during the Bush years; in area after area of American life you can find a steadiness, a predictability, that speaks of circumscription, yes, but also paradoxically of permissiveness, the one leading to the other.

In those footling examples from my own life, the lesson is clear and again harks back to the balance early Americans had to make between rugged independence and the need to be their neighbours' keepers in a hostile environment that could pick off individuals all too easily. Europeans tend to think of cradle-to-grave safety nets as being very much their province and broadly speaking that's true; there is an ideological commitment to social action and social control in

Europe that Americans simply do not share. But Americans are perfectly capable of collective action, enforced by the government, when they see the need and in particular when the benefits are readily visible to all segments of society, including those at the top. Hence the rules that we encountered in our suburban street: an interest in road safety, in a nation not short of roads, is an American no-brainer.

Turn your mind back to the trial of Zacarias Moussaoui – a trial that ended with a surprise. Moussaoui was the man regarded by the Bush administration as the "twentieth hijacker" – a man who was intimately involved with the 9/11 plot. Moussaoui himself confirmed that charge – gloried in it. In court, they called relatives of the victims as witnesses. They played tapes of people's last calls home. It was a devastating, emotional case and all of it was presented to jurors who lived within miles of the Pentagon. Their response fascinated me. They looked at the case and gradually, over several days, they picked it apart. They cried when the victims' relatives cried. They looked ashen-faced when a video was shown of people jumping to their deaths from the twin towers. But they followed the rules – which in this case said that they needed to be sure Moussaoui shared responsibility for all this suffering. And at least one of the jury members decided – against the weight of expectation of an entire nation – that he did not. Moussaoui was a liar and a fantasist and should not be executed. Even if the President desired it. Even if their gut instinct was to order it.

In the days after the verdict, the brilliant and perceptive

former Reagan speechwriter Peggy Noonan wrote in the *Wall Street Journal* that the jurors had made a mistake, treating the legal niceties of the Moussaoui case with "a daintiness" that spoke of weakness. She has a point. To many Americans, the whole notion of using the courts to combat Islamic crazies reeks of suicide, of giving up. But of course it isn't: the Moussaoui verdict was the opposite of giving up. What the Moussaoui jury did was strike a blow for a fundamental tenet of American freedom. The man had his day in court and the degree of culpability for the crimes of which he was accused was dispassionately weighed by a jury that took its duties seriously. In fact, his day in court became weeks and then months, and during that time he was allowed to speak his mind. His trial was fair. He was not hanged from a lamp-post however much the nation at large might have seen that as his just desert. And although anti-Americans use Guantanamo Bay as an example of the fundamental inability of the USA to be serious about its commitment to human rights., the opposite is the case.

Guantanamo was a disaster for the Bush administration because of home-grown protest. Amnesty International they could have coped with. The Council of Europe they could safely have ignored. Foreign public opinion as well. It has been the relentless drip drip of American legal opinions, including those of the Supreme Court itself, that has under-cut the ability of the Bush team to do what they wanted to do at Guantanamo. Even the European attack, led by the Swiss MP Dick Marty, relied on US news reports for its evidence of US wrongdoing. It was the *Washington Post* – an American institution in every sense of the word – that reported the CIA was "hiding and interrogating some of its most important al-Qaeda captives at a Soviet-era compound in Eastern Europe".

Dainty lawyers and dainty reporters trumped a president in his pomp in the midst of a war. For all the power that the Bush White House accrued to itself, for all the intentions it had to fight the war with radical Islam in semi-legal shadows, the upshot has been row after row with Americans who will not stand for this behaviour in their name. And in 2008 they choose two presidential candidates, *both of whom* were genuinely implacably opposed to torture, both in name and in fact. Guantanamo Bay was ordered into existence by America and ordered out as well. Some of President Bush's critics worried in the years after 2001 whether the US had lost touch with its soul. One, the writer Naomi Wolf, thought she could smell fascism, but it seems to me that America is on the way to re-finding its central core.

That core is individualism. A love of the essence of America is a love of freedom but a love too of the rules that make the nation free. And boy, is it a love that dares to speak its name. In fact, it dares to *shout* it in a way that leads the anti-American crowd to suggest that the very keenness of Americans to boast about their freedom is a sign of their brainwashed state. Ever since de Tocqueville delivered his magisterial verdict on American democracy ("good in parts" is a fair summary), outsiders have been whinging about

American trumpet blowing. Jonathan Freedland has written wisely of the way in which innocent pride gets mistaken for jingoism, particularly in the repetition of the simple word America as in *America's Most Wanted* or *America's Funniest Home Videos*. I have an update trumping even those TV shows: when the Governor of New Jersey, James McGreevey, announced to a wondrous nation, with his long-suffering wife at his side, that he was resigning after having had an adulterous affair with a man, he used this telling formulation: "And so, my truth is that I am a gay American."

A gay *American*. It softens the blow. It reminds the nation of the impulse towards inclusiveness that is at its core. Italian Americans, once downtrodden now mainstream. Ditto German Americans or Japanese Americans or Chinese Americans. Let us hear it – the Governor seemed to be saying – for married, gay, American governors who have let down their families in humiliating circumstances. Yippee! Nice try, I say: only in America is the McGreevey effort even conceivable.

And as for more conventional protestations of patriotism, again Freedland had it right when, ten years ago, he used the phrase "the patriotism of common purpose". A lot has happened to America since then, much of it not good, but the phrase is still a meaningful one. Even post-9/11, the chest-beating patriotism, the nationalism of a wounded nation in the mood to get in the faces of the rest of the world, has been the exception not the rule.

And too often outsiders confuse American patriotism

with a love of, and a respect for, the state itself – in fact, the opposite is the case. America's self-love is, by and large, a wholesome thing. America's self-love is, by and large, a wholesome thing. The soldiers at Barack Obama's inauguration were dressed in nineteenth century gear. The parade was of floats representing school dancing bands, not army regiments. Every July the Fourth, I go with my family to a parade on the outskirts of Washington. There is of course an official celebration in the middle of town, with fireworks and celebrities and speaker systems and security. But our parade is the authentic face of the Fourth, the same face seen in a hundred thousand American towns on that day, with the volunteer fire department taking part, local businesses distributing sweets, local politicians hoping to make friends.

Our parade, usually taking place under the intense early summer sun, is a joyful mess. Children rush between the dance troupes, the veteran car drivers and the school bands. Everywhere there is music and sweets and flags. Flags! To British eyes, the nearest equivalent is the visit of the Queen to a little market town in the West Country, a visit that will have been preceded by the scrubbing of the streets and the ejection of the destitute. But our eyes deceive us. Our sense of what is happening on July the Fourth on main streets around the nation is fundamentally wrong. Those little flags which Americans wave are not doing the job that the Union flags do when the Royal Family come visiting Giggleswick.

The Union Jacks show allegiance to the Queen, to the

system. The graffiti on the wall of the local school has been cleaned up so that Her Majesty might not be displeased, and the village shamed. On one such visit to the city of Bath, Queen Victoria felt she had been slighted by the locals and on subsequent train journeys past the city she used to order the blinds to be drawn. No such relationship exists between American presidents and American cities. Important national days here are a celebration of the lives *of those doing the celebrating*. What Americans celebrate is *their* power over the State, their allegiance to themselves. They are not waving their flags for the president, even when the president is popular; still less for Congress or the Supreme Court. They are celebrating their own power. A power protected above all by laws and judicial systems that can operate independently even in the most difficult circumstances. A judicial system that can bounce back and throughout the history of the United States has bitten the legs of those who think they might have trampled it. One that survived President Bush, not through its intellectual power or through force of arms or even through control of the rules, but for a deeper, visceral reason: because Americans like the idea that they are free. Yes, it is in part a myth, but they like the myth so much they have, in the words of that iconic American advertisement, bought the company. They are shareholders and like all shareholders they value their investment.

But what does that mean for the rest of us? One of the greatest foreign myths of recent times has been the widely touted view that the United States is a nation with an overriding purpose and that purpose is to screw us and enrich them. Is there not ample evidence?

No, actually. Or at least not evidence of conscious imperialism of the British or Roman stripe. Nor is there evidence of an imperialism that enriches only the imperial power. In fact, the opposite: evidence of an American worldview that makes even a disguised version of American imperialism a tricky proposition to sell to most Americans.

A short holiday brought it home to me. Our letter of introduction needed to be above suspicion. Forgeries had been attempted in the past, so this single side of A4 had been notarised – approved and stamped by a solicitor – before being sent to us, along with instructions and further documentation. In some parts of the world, there'd be less fuss involved in buying a house or adopting a child, but in this corner of America all we were trying to do was get onto the beach. I am standing in a car park, within earshot though not yet sight of the ocean, and negotiating a day's visit with a friendly but watchful official whose job is to keep the riff-raff out.

"I'm Ted," he says. "We haven't met." He has a firm handshake and the general demeanour of a friendly police inspector, a person from whom you have nothing to fear unless, that is, you have done something wrong.

We have come to the Hamptons, a string of exclusive villages, whose architectural style suggests a kind of rustic idyll on steroids. The Hamptons are very close to Manhattan, no more than a couple of hours by car, or on one of the luxury buses that ply the route (the only example in the whole of the United States of public transport being cool) and a good deal less in the executive jet. The consequence of this proximity is that many wealthy New Yorkers live here for at least some of the year.

The evening we arrived, I had driven out to find a shop and taken a wrong turn down a road which could have been a disused movie set. Every hundred metres or so, a gravel drive led up to a huge and pristine mansion, apparently built or rebuilt within the last few years, with shingle siding, neat wooden decking, freshly painted pools gated and covered, manicured lawns and – a nice touch this – many of them boasting those swings that hang from the branches of large trees, giving a kind of *faux* casualness, a 1950s "gosh we don't need much to enjoy ourselves" feel, in the corner of a lifestyle statement which says the very opposite.

I had to peer about in the light of the full moon to see all this, though, because another feature of the Hamptons is that all the best bits are populated by people for whom a house here is just one of many. If you're visiting off-season, as I was, most of the owners are elsewhere, their Gatsby mansions dark.

On the first day of our family holiday we had driven to see something that counts in these parts as pretty ancient history. In the nineteenth century, Sag Harbour was a busy whaling town: now it's a slightly over-clean tourist trap with a marina. Where once there might have been doss-houses and brothels, there are now impossibly exclusive florists and a second-hand bookshop specialising in first editions. We eat on picnic tables overlooking the boats; no longer whalers covered in blood and blubber, of course, but an altogether different boating scene, in which specks of dust are being removed from teak deck furniture by uniformed flunkies.

As we munch and take in the scene, a man with a child a similar age to ours smiles at my wife Sarah and asks, "Weren't you at the Shirtlers' party?" Alas, we were not, but in this place, when the sun shines, all the world is a party and all the men and women merely partygoers. It is a bit unreal. And, as my father-in-law Charlie remarked as we got ready to leave, it's a long, long way from Baghdad. That comment was revealing, I thought, in a way that he didn't quite intend. Of course the Hamptons are a long way from Baghdad; but how interesting that Charlie could think for a minute that that might not have been the case. Somewhere in his mind he plainly (and not unreasonably) associated America with America's actions abroad and assumed, however fleetingly, that the war would have some kind of visible impact at home. Assumed, perhaps, that the Hamptons would be abuzz with news from the front as in his youth, when wealthy folk in country houses in the 'Shires would have dismissed the maid and gathered around the wireless to hear the BBC bringing news of bombing missions in Germany. Assumed that a nation with global reach and global responsibilities would have found a modern equivalent of melting down the iron railings for the war effort. Assumed that America was serious about what others have decided is its imperial role.

Not here it isn't. In the Hamptons, a battle is being waged, but it certainly isn't with global terrorism. The battle is essentially a class war, the "haves" keeping out the "have lesses". Back at the seafront, we hand over photo IDs provided by the owners of the house we are borrowing; our English accents convince Ted the gatekeeper that a minor issue about the transferability of the car park pass can be overlooked, and finally we gain access to the seaside. A boardwalk takes us up to the summit of the sand dune and we look over it at the water and the beach. We are the only people here. On either side the sands stretch, the waves crash, and there is solitude.

Again the exceptionalism created by space. The space, in this case, to ignore the siren call of global domination. To be sure, the Hamptons, snooty, dressy, exclusive, far from Baghdad, are an anomaly. But here is an odd fact of 21st-century life that the Hamptons epitomise: America is a nation that has stumbled into a position of global leadership, global domination, without the elites at home really being the slightest bit interested, at least not in the sense of accepting personal sacrifice, personal responsibility. America is at war – America is leading a global war – but with pockets of the nation, important pockets, leadership pockets, apparently unaffected, undisturbed.

On a summer night, just as the heat was starting to take its toll on Washington, I was at the house of David

Frum, the former Bush speechwriter. A tropical rain storm coincided with this party, so we crammed into a screened porch (an anteroom open to the outside world except for a thin layer of wire mesh to keep the bugs out). As the ceiling fans whirred above us, we heard from a Frum friend, a fellow right-wing intellectual who had just written a book about the history of the idea of honour. Whilst sweat dripped off our noses and into our champagne glasses, Frum gave a speech endorsing his friend and his book and ending with this thought: that the author's association with honour was all the more striking and real because he had a son, and I remember this phrase, with its old-fashioned ring, "serving gallantly in Iraq".

There was intense applause, out of support no doubt, out of sympathy perhaps; but mostly because the audience was genuinely moved, I think, that here, in one of the most privileged of American settings, within sight of a simply stunning outdoor pool, at the back of a gorgeous, generously-proportioned house, was a man, the author, who was actually connected to the fighting. A man who was not, in my father-in-law's words, a long way from Baghdad. A man who must have winced inside every time he heard of American casualties – at this stage of the war, almost every day. A man whose family is doing its bit for an effort that began (how easy it is to forget this or to hide it) with genuine nationwide support.

But here's the reason that moment so stuck in my mind: it was terribly unusual. In fact, in my experience unique. To many Americans it is shocking that those involved at the sharp end of US foreign policy are unrelated, literally, to those who give the orders, or at least vote to give permission for war to begin.

Only a few years ago, according to the US Retired Officers Association, it would have been unthinkable to suggest that Congress and the military were growing apart. Every year from 1951 to 1992, more than 50 per cent of the members of Congress were veterans. The peak for veterans in Congress came during 1977–78, when 77 per cent of the lawmakers had military experience. In times of war, most of their children were thrown into battle. Now it is optional. Deeply optional. One or two have a personal stake in the Iraq War (the sons of John McCain and the Democratic Senator Jim Webb are prominent exceptions to the "kids don't serve" rule), and around election time large numbers of congressmen made trips to Baghdad, but the conquest of Iraq was not led by America's ruling class. They wanted little part in it.

Questions about America's commitment to imperial ventures go much wider than the simple issue of whether the sons and daughters of the powerful serve in the military. The "white man's burden" that Americans are accused of seeking and claiming requires a conquest mindset. I am not sure the Americans have it.

A few years ago, the British historian Niall Ferguson wrote *Colossus: The Rise and Fall of the American Empire*, a book that caused quite a stir in the United States: he suggested that America was an imperial power (not a hugely controversial idea) but he went further, suggesting a) that this was broadly speaking a good thing, and b) that Americans needed to adjust their own behaviour at home, namely banish imperial denial, to take account of their new global responsibilities. He asked whether America was, in a memorable phrase, *a strategic couch potato*. His conclusion was that it needn't be: that although Americans are often physically fat and mentally lazy, they might still be able to sort themselves out.

I think the jury is out. And if eventually the verdict of history is that early 21st-century America *was* an imperial power, it will stretch beyond breaking point any realistic definition of what imperialism is. Remember, Iraq was sold to the American people as self-defence. When the former White House Press Secretary Scott McClellan attacked the administration for what he claimed was its use of propaganda to justify the Iraq War, he made the telling point that the real driving force behind the policy – a desire among some neoconservatives to rebuild the Middle East – could never have been used as the public justification for the invasion. Even after the weapons of mass destruction failed to materialise, it was vital that the American people be told that the war was a war *to defend the homeland*. This fabrication upset McClellan, who went home to Texas and wrote a book attacking the duplicity involved in making this case. Since he sat through the whole of the war in the Bush White House, apparently happy with what he saw and heard, he is not necessarily the strongest witness. But on this issue he is right. There was a deception and the deception was vital. There are no votes in American imperialism.

There are plenty of votes in American self-confidence, however. This self-confidence is at the heart of America's world domination, a self-confidence which frankly should not alarm anyone. America is not imperial in the classic sense, but Americans certainly believe in the universality of their national myth, of their core beliefs. If you are going to project power around the world, if you want your system of government, or something approximating it, to be everyone's way of doing things, it does help to stay off the introspection and self-doubt. There are, of course, many introspective Americans (Woody Allen?) but there is a national consensus summed up in the Declaration of Independence itself: "life, liberty, and the pursuit of happiness". That final phrase translated to modern life: being relaxed; chilling.

Americans are a driven people but they relax with the same passion they take to work. They are not fussed enough about the world to want to keep it in order for long. In spite of the religiously inspired work ethic and the crazy commuters driving long hours every day to keep bread on their family table, in spite of all the well-documented activist frenzy of American life, the purpose – the ultimate purpose – is still *having some fun*. Taking it easy. That is what Americans are buying with their sweat. Go back to the Fourth of July, Independence Day. Just as the old Soviet May Day military parades showed the weakness of the state:

all that oppressive hardware, unyielding and inhumane; so the casualness of the American Independence Day experience seems to me to reveal the strength of this nation. We are often reminded of how well we Brits do formal ceremonies. Is that anything to be proud of? The Americans are awful at them; a sign, it seems to me, of the reality of America's unimperial core.

I remember watching the traditional procession from Congress back to the White House after the Bush second-term inauguration. The President and Dick Cheney could hardly keep still in their bulletproof box, chatting and backslapping, and was it my imagination or did the Vice President actually take out a disposable camera and get a couple of shots for his collection? They did not take themselves too seriously anyway; in fact, part of the Bush genius was to tap into this rich seam of unaffected American casualness in a way neither Al Gore nor John Kerry could ever manage, a casualness that speaks not of overbearing imperialism, but of homespun incompetence. Obama's first few days in the White House were the same: the order to close Guantanamo Bay was signed in a chaos of photographers and junior staff working out which documents went where.

Look at the utter disaster the White House made of the welcome of the Chinese President a few years ago. The visit had been in planning since the Ming Dynasty, but when it came to it, the casual Americans allowed a protester to get in, and announced their Chinese host as the President of the Republic of China (that's Taiwan, which the Chinese regard as a renegade illegitimate breakaway state. China is the *People's* Republic). I was standing next to an English sino-logist who was almost physically sick at the enormity of the error.

But hey, the locals didn't care. This is America. This is the centre of the world. Taiwan, China, whatever. And this was not, of course, a one-off error. I remember flying to Belfast with the Bush White House team, and being handed a pro-gramme of events entitled "Visit of the President and Mrs Bush to Ireland". Actually the visit was only to Northern Ireland, a distinction which had been famously regarded as rather important by the locals but which the White House felt able airily to ignore. And the Unionist politicians on that occasion showed us all how to react to this tendency. Even this prickly bunch saw the funny side of it, saw that this mindset did not speak of hostility, but of distance and geography, of an isolation from the details of other people's conflicts that hails from the size of the great plains, from the distances and rhythms of American life, from the fact that in so much of America abroad is such a long way away.

So might the rest of us occasionally have to grit our teeth as our statesmen and women are disrespected and our heritage unwittingly belittled by Washington? Yes, 'fraid so; we should, to use a wonderful American expression, suck it up. America's absent-minded approach to the world is often cited as an example of its miserable ignorance and incompe-tence which results in great damage (think of *The Quiet American* by Graham Greene) and it is difficult to deny that a more nuanced knowledge of the details of Iraqi life and culture might have prevented a catastrophe for that nation and for Americans from unfolding in the years after 2003. But this failure, if true failure it is, cannot be cited alongside the charge of imperialism. America should not be accused one minute of planning world domination, and the next minute of failing to have the foggiest idea about what it is doing. If you want to make the case against America, you have to choose. But you do not have to try to force the issue. You can abstain and give the Yanks the benefit of the doubt. In the broad sweep of history, America has spent most of its life, and will spend most of its life in the future, defending its domestic freedom and hoping hard that others will admire and respect it, but not forcing the issue.

If this mighty war machine, this mighty commercial engine, this uniquely robust place were truly to have a go at studying the rest of us and taking us over, they would make quick work of it. It would be like a Hollywood film, with us as the earthlings and them the four-headed computer-driven monsters arriving in space capsules. Only there would be no happy ending. They would win. But they have no such intentions. We are safe. Phew.

Of course Americans care more about their own freedom than anyone else's. That is because they are human beings and like all human beings they have a tendency to look after themselves and their own. Barack Obama's patriotism is as profound as any of his countrymen and women. But their desire to protect their way of life does not result in slavery for the rest of us. America will not take over the world; Americans would not stand for it.

6. Religion

OVER THE YEARS, a rich seam of "evidence" for the ghastliness of the United States has been found in the madness and/or the badness of the religious right, whose behaviour, as reported in the British press, places America politically somewhere between the faeries and the Taliban. Later, in my chapter on the deepest of American vices, religion plays a starring role because there is simply no question that some aspects of the nation's religious life do real damage to the ability of individual Americans to think straight. But there is more to this story.

There is a local newspaper group in Illinois whose motto reads: "To fear God, tell the truth and make money." To many outsiders, America, in its religious life, has concentrated way too hard on the first and the last of those more or less admirable aims. Truth, in the sense of dispassionate exploration of ideas, in the great tradition of philosophy and theology, has been the first casualty. The Devil has had a field day.

We Europeans all know what we think of American Christian fundamentalism, and prominent fundamentalists; although the real loonies are often not the best known. One of my favourites was the Reverend Carl McIntyre, whose obituary in the *Daily Telegraph* did not beat about the bush:

> In his one-man bid to reverse the 20th century's moral decline, McIntyre opposed evolution, sex education, the civil rights movement and fluoridated water. Comet Kahoutek, he proclaimed, marked the Second Coming, and he assembled a panel to determine whether creatures in UFOs resembled beings described in the Book of Revelation. McIntyre's broadcasts attracted up to 4,000 letters a day and, by some estimates, \$4 million a year in donations. His motto was: "A man who will not use his freedom to defend his freedom does not deserve his freedom", and in 1948 he argued that America had a moral duty to launch a nuclear strike on the Soviet Union.

And yet...

It's five in the morning and I am driving home through the Washington suburbs for an hour or so in bed before returning to the office. The date: November 4th, 2006 – actually the early hours of November 5th – the date that the Bush administration received official confirmation from the American people that they despised it and wished it gone. The mid-term elections that year did not involve Mr Bush personally but they certainly involved his party and his failing political powers; in the hours before my trip home, we had been reporting on a catastrophic night for the

Republicans – they lost power in both houses of Congress, the Senate and the House of Representatives – and with those losses, the White House also lost the power to govern without first seeking the approval or the acquiescence of the opposition Democrats. A more wily president, a nimbler character, might have made it work, but the Bush demise was written in his genes; he couldn't hack compromise. The 2006 election was the beginning of the end.

I drove with the roof down. It's that weird weather again, that never-quite-to-be-trusted American weather that speaks of danger and opportunity. November, a month of winter chill in the UK as I remember it, can be Washington's finest time. The temperatures veer crazily from sub-zero to T-shirt heat. At nightfall in Britain we are used to a gradual cooling, an autumnal chill that sets in some time in October. Here the opposite is often the case: cold, wet days will become suddenly tropically hot; the pavements literally steaming in the glare of early evening headlamps. And everywhere and in all temperatures and conditions the trees become huge beacons of colour: reds and yellows and russets, glinting in the sunshine. When it rains, the overhead canopy weeps prettily and constantly. A tree-lined avenue close to my home, free of traffic at this early hour, is like a Manhattan ticker-tape parade, only more colourful; tens of thousands of leaves drifting lazily through the air from what appears at times to be a limitless supply. Danger and opportunity.

As I speed through this perfect American moment, this film-set backdrop, I feel two things. First, happy to live here in a nation where real change can be wrought by the electorate, and no army comes out of the barracks to stop it; you can get home without bumping into any tanks. And secondly, angry at the cynics and charlatans, the thugs and friends of thugs around the world, who suggest that American democracy is a sham – that real choices are not made here, real opinions not honed by independent people. Long before the drama of 2008, long before the campaign and the big choices the world watched, this had been a night that had served as proof for me that American democracy exists – it *functions* – and the proof was in the destruction, the outright annihilation, of the power of the social conservatives, the religious right.

A thumping the President called it – good old George did have a way with words describing physical violence – and a thumping it was. The thumping delivered the first ever defeat – in the state of Arizona – of a state ballot initiative that would have banned gay marriage. In rural South Dakota, a measure outlawing abortion under almost all circumstances was also defeated. And in the conservative heartland, Missouri, state funding of stem cell research was approved. But the other killer blow to social conservatism's political potency was its adoption, at least in moderated form, by the Democrats – in key states they fielded candidates who were *not* keen on abortion, *not* keen on gay rights. These candidates were immune to attacks from the social conservatives, because they were conservative themselves, but they wore their conservatism lightly; they

135

were not on board for a political effort to get gay marriage banned and abortion severely curtailed. They had other priorities. The result of this: Americans were freed from the terrible stress of the "culture war" that has raged on and off in the United States since the 1970s. Instead, they voted on issues any European could recognise as properly political: corruption, Iraq, the economy. They did it again in 2008 in large measure, but the trend was started two years earlier.

In the days after the mid-terms, Mr Bush did his best to pick himself up off the deck, brush himself down like a true Texan and get on with life. But something had happened that he did not see coming; and to be fair he was not alone. The early years of this century saw book after book on the subject of the triumph of America's religiously inspired social conservatism. They certainly convinced Karl Rove, the man they called Bush's brain, the principal architect of both his presidential victories. He talked of creating a governing majority, a long-term Republican Party ascendancy based on the pillar of religion or of religious people.

But the books were wrong. The thesis that activists on the right, bolstered by religious bigots, would rule America for the foreseeable future has died a death. Americans have not become more European and nor should wise Europeans yearn for that outcome; but Americans have shown their true colours when it comes to matters relating to religion and freedom, and those colours are vivid and fascinating and worthy of respect.

Religious conservatism is plainly a principal cause of suspicion and distrust between Europe and America, but fair-minded Europeans should accept that America is changing.

Why this change? What happened? Many years ago, the British historian George Dangerfield wrote a work that became a classic: *The Strange Death of Liberal England.* Dangerfield's subject was the sudden and totally unexpected demise of Edwardian social mores and political certainties, a demise which came at what appeared to be the zenith of Edwardianism, when threats seemed miniscule and prospects heroically assured. In 2006, we witnessed the strange death of socially conservative America – or to be more precise the death of social conservatism – focusing on abortion and homosexuality and other such personal moral issues – as *the* decisive factor in American politics. Values voters, so called, had won it for George in 2000 (just) and in 2004 (quite easily). They had been on a roll. Again the threats were miniscule or seemed to be so. American atheists were nowhere to be seen. The Democrats were visible but at sea. And yet the conservatives blew it, and the manner in which they did this was spectacular and should be studied hard by anyone who wants to understand America, to give the place a chance. Actually, it should be studied by the haters as well, though they may be too preoccupied with moaning about evangelicals to get to grips with the truth.

Part of the reason for this strange death was that Americans – particularly suburban Americans – decided the religious right had gone too far. They would have seen the ludicrous spectacle days before the 2006 election of a very well-known evangelical preacher named Ted Haggard – a self-proclaimed White House advisor – having to admit that he had bought drugs and enjoyed a rubdown from a gay masseur; a massage he had received during a short break from his lectures to the nation on the dangers of gay marriage. This was a handy reminder to normal Americans that private lives are often complicated. But it was more: it was a reminder as well that this land is known – and not ironically in these parts – as the land of the free. American freedom really does count for something. It is in the DNA; and the social conservatives forgot.

At my twins' annual school camp in West Virginia, you are meant to leave your troubles behind. It is an idyllic couple of days – a communing with nature that my wife gallantly insists is simply too enjoyable for her to take part in – it has to be a dad's experience. Actually it's not that uncomfortable – the tents are like those of an army in the field, sensible structures with plenty of room to stand up in, and rudimentary bunk beds you can bang your head on in the early morning. The setting is a reminder of the size of the United States – only two hours from the nation's capital, these are woods and fields as spacious and far-flung as the Scottish Highlands. My kids love it – they and twenty other seven year olds roast marshmallows by the campfire, catch tadpoles in the pond, and roam around, unwashed, at five in the morning in the early light of the West Virginia day, pointing their torches into each other's tents. "Did Cole sleep in his dad's car?" "Did Peter's water bottle break?"

"Did Rachel's mum fall out of bed?" etc etc. And then comes breakfast. Breakfast is an indoors affair – not luxurious but hey, this is America and these are middle-class kids and some parents are beginning to flag by seven in the morning and need the familiar comforts of multi-coloured cereals and soy milk.

First though – a silence. Please take off your hats, asks the cheery camp counsellor (yes, that's what they call them). She looks down, then up again. The silence lasts less than a minute, after which my daughter Martha discovers that there are pancakes with M&Ms inside them to eat and we give the silence not another thought. But I am a foreigner here, an anthropologist in a largely friendly tribe, and one of the pitfalls of anthropology is that there are some things you have to be a member of the tribe to really *get*. Unbeknownst to me, the silence has caused outrage – or to be more precise, has caused great delight to some and great outrage to others. I discover this later when talking to a dad about the post-silence debate which took place between certain concerned parents and the silence-enforcing camp counsellor.

Basically the problem is this: what was the silence? What was it *for*? Was it contemplative or was it religious?

The distinction to my English mind was unimportant – English people tend not to be religious, it is true, but we are not overly fussed about the trappings of religion in the public space. To us it is background noise, no big deal. But in modern America it is a huge deal. Some parents believed that the Breakfast Silence was an attempt by a religious cabal to take over our camp – to insinuate their beliefs into our get-together, to steal the minds of our kids. Are they right to be in such a funk? I am not sure that they are. The religious intolerance and the downright foolishness of much of America's religious experience is, it seems to me, impossible to deny. And yet, try as they might, the real enthusiasts for theocracy repeatedly fail to get their ideas to fly. When you visit them – as I did, coincidentally, just days after the Breakfast Silence issue – you find a group of people in a funk comparable to that of the atheists.

On the face of it, creationism, albeit disguised as something called Intelligent Design, is on the march in modern America. A number of Americans appear to have trouble grasping evolution. After years of quiescence, the creationist movement is trying to get its hands on school-kids in several states, and create the impression that Darwinism is controversial. Like many small but well-organised lobby groups, the movement packs a punch. And the Creation Museum, a short taxi ride from the rational world of Cincinnati Airport, is intended to be the leading edge of the glove. It is a wonderfully American place, carved into the Kentucky countryside, hugely well endowed with parking and snack facilities. It is light and spacious and – why did I find this surprising? – rather fashionable-looking, not your grandmother's creationist museum.

I was there in Kentucky the day after it opened; a moment evangelicals should really have been celebrating with great gusto. To an extent they were. The museum is a striking place, with wonderfully lifelike models of Adam and Eve (Eve almost erotic, with her hair arranged to cover her nakedness) and an airy, well-put-together feel. But I didn't get the impression from those in charge or those visiting that they felt themselves to be on the march in modern America. In fact, the whole thing had a slightly beleaguered feel. One parent confided, "At last there's a place I can bring the kids where they are taught what we teach them at home." Another asked me almost plaintively whether I was convinced by the museum's planetarium where the sun was created after the earth. I had to be honest and say that I wasn't, but I felt quite sorry as I did – there is nothing remotely convincing about the Creation Museum and frankly, if it poses the threat to the science base of America that some American critics claim it does, that seems to me to be as much a commentary on their failings as on those of the creationists.

There is a reason why theocracy will never fly in the United States and it's been touched on, inadvertently, by George Bush himself. Mr Bush was fond of making the point that the philosophy of the Islamic radicals, full of hate and oppression, would not be attractive to people who truly had the freedom to choose. Similarly, the philosophy of the Old Testament – so much celebrated by some evangelicals here – has a limited power to enthral free people. At the Creation Museum goggle-eyed children watch depictions of the Great Flood – in which children and their mums and dads are consumed, because God is cross. In a nation of kindly, moderate people, I'm not sure these ideas can ever really catch on. Yes, they tell opinion polls in depressingly large numbers that they think the earth was created recently by a chap with a beard. But they do not follow through. They are too good. They went to the brink with Bush and when they got there, they decided to turn back.

And they turned back long before Barack Obama came along with his Bible-free second oath – after the first one, on Inauguration Day, was messed up when the Chief Justice got the words wrong – his enthusiasm for embryonic stem cell research and his insouciance about paying US dollars to aid agencies that give abortion advice. No, they had already turned back and the cause was not Obama and his rhetoric; the cause was freedom.

If there was one event that set this new course, this course we should all be noticing and respecting, it was probably the fight over the body, and the brain, of Terri Schiavo, a fight that would involve President Bush, in his pyjamas, the social conservatives on their high horses, and the courts in the role the founding fathers intended, calming the mob.

On the morning of February 25th, 1990, Terri Schiavo, an insurance claims clerk living in St Petersburg, Florida, collapsed on the floor of the apartment she shared with her husband Michael. She had suffered a heart attack, possibly brought on by the effects of eating disorders. She was 27. Paramedics said they found her face down and unconscious. Early efforts to resuscitate her came to nothing; by the time she was breathing again, her brain had been damaged beyond rescue. But she was not dead. Doctors, including several neurologists, diagnosed a persistent vegetative state: Terri was not going to get better. But, fed through tubes, she was not going to die. It was a tragedy, but a tragedy that touched only one family. It did not appear to have any national significance, still less any political weight. Even when Michael Schiavo, Terri's husband, decided it was time for the court to rule on whether his wife's feeding tubes should be withdrawn, and a legal battle began between him and the woman's parents, there was little publicity. The courts decided that Terri Schiavo had made "credible and reliable" statements in the past indicating that she would not want to be kept alive indefinitely under these circumstances. They sided with Michael Schiavo.

And that is the moment the Terri Schiavo case was seized on by social conservatives. Of course, many of them – including the parents Robert and Mary Schindler – genuinely believed that their case had merits; that a living woman should be kept alive. The American religious right gets a bad press in Europe because Europeans hear too much about the nutters and not enough about the gentle faithful, the prison visitors and hot-meal providers. I am certainly not suggesting that those who opposed the courts in the Terri Schiavo case were all extremists on a mission. But as the court battle went on and the years rolled by, for every simply good-hearted believer in life, there were a dozen campaigners and political hacks joining up to make a wider point: to win a battle for Jesus and for His Chosen Party, the

Republicans. One over-zealous Republican senator's aide was so fired up by Terri Schiavo that he committed himself to print, writing in a memo to his boss, Mel Martinez of Florida, that the case was "a great political issue" that would appeal to the party grass-roots.

Well it was, wasn't it? How could that party aide have known that Terri Schiavo would soon be dead, that he would soon be fired, and that his party would be torn apart? Had not America just re-elected an evangelical president, backed by majorities in both Houses of Congress? Were not the leaders of the Republicans in both those Houses (Bill Frist and Tom DeLay) 100-per-cent born again? Hadn't opposition to gay marriage been a crucial issue in 2004? Wasn't faith-based politics at the very zenith of its power at home and even abroad? Hadn't a crusade against those Mr Bush called "evil doers" seen early successes in Afghanistan and begun quite promisingly in Iraq? (Remember that "Mission Accomplished" didn't look ridiculous on the day.)

What happened next illustrates my point that America is a complex and often surprising place. Tiring of losing battle after battle in the Florida courts, the Schiavo campaigners turned to the big guns in Congress. First, they persuaded a congressional committee to subpoena Michael and Terri Schiavo to appear before them in Washington; since it is a serious offence to interfere with such a demand, the thinking went that Terri Schiavo could not be allowed to die while the subpoena was in force. At this stage it still felt to many (and I must confess I was one of them) that the courts were going to get a beating from a movement on the march. So when a judge struck down the subpoena, there was talk of impeaching him for the crime of being "arrogant and out of control". In the meantime on Capitol Hill, a new approach was taken: a private bill was passed (without any opposition in the Senate – that's how steamrollerish this all felt) transferring Terri Schiavo's future out of the Florida legal system and into the federal courts. The President flew back across the country from his holiday home in Texas to sleep at the White House for one night and to be woken in the early hours to sign the legislation. He did so, in his pyjamas, at 1.11am on March 21st, 2005.

Surely now the moment had come for the faithful to taste victory. The 24-hour TV news shows went into hyperdrive (overdrive is for wars or US elections; hyperdrive for something really special) with non-stop emotive coverage of "Terri" looking responsive, affectionate, vulnerable. This was the moment for the USA to be defined for the new century as a post-industrial society with a difference; the only advanced nation on earth where God was smiting his foes with mighty force. A place where democracy really does take second place to religion, where the visceral call of faith trumps the rational mind. But the federal courts – impressed by the scientists who said Terri Schiavo was incapable of getting better and unimpressed by the call of faith alone – backed the Florida judges. The Supreme Court collectively yawned and raised an eyebrow; the justices refused even to hear the case. Terri Schiavo's feeding tubes

145

were removed and she died on March 31st, 2005. And America did not rise up against the judges, in fact, in opinion poll after opinion poll a firm majority of the American people calmly sided with Terri Schiavo's husband and with the courts: America, God fearing as it is, faithful as her inhabitants are, is a nation of lawyers, and I mean this in a good way. The founding fathers decided that, in the world's first democratic country, the powers of the government would be limited; this term has a rather unworldly academic feeling, but in application it is rather simple: if you can convince the courts that you are in the right, then no politician, no majority in Congress, no president in or out of his pyjamas, can stop you. Americans, in the latest of their periodic religious convulsions, had got rather used to the idea that rules about private matters could be made and enforced by politicians fuelled by faith. But when they got to the edge of the theocratic canyon, they peered down, felt queasy and pulled back. Quite simply the President had overreached himself. So had the two men who led the Republicans in each of the two Houses of Congress (both are now out of politics) and so had the religious conservatives who sought to intervene in what most Americans regarded as a private matter and one that might genuinely concern them and their families. The nation was asked to go on a crusade but instead chose to see a lawyer and make a living will.

To those who carp on about the religious right and its supposed sway over American public life, I say: look at the facts. Yes, there are a large number of people in Washington for whom the rational world appears oddly distant – as I acknowledge elsewhere in the book – but the nation at large is not in their thrall because the nation at large takes its freedom seriously. We are back to the geography; the space, the political set-up arranged to persuade prickly independent-minded people living far away from each other that common cause does not equal enslavement.

"Don't pick up hitchhikers!" the roadside signs warn. We are getting close to the Tucker Correctional Facility, set in the middle of the flat Arkansas countryside. Disappointed with the creationists, I have come to observe yet another of those religious infringements on public life that seem to suggest that America is irredeemably odd, or crazy, or unknowable; that the place cannot be considered to be truly civilised. Again, the physical harshness of the environment hits you first: the June heat is body-sapping, the sun unfriendly and unrelenting. The car's air-conditioning struggles to cope; only a madman, or an escaping felon, would hitchhike here. In fact, only a madman would stand around doing anything in the Arkansas countryside in the summer; the mosquitoes are the size of parrots (well, almost) – you could bleed to death. At night if you drive fast, you see a stream of them in the beam of the headlamps, a fog of discomfort. Life in Arkansas – the Barefoot State – has always been pretty tough. As so often in America, the natural environment is harsh but can be stunningly beautiful. Man's contribution, however, is pretty ropey: ghastly shacks and rusting vehicles bequeathed by generations of humans who have lived here as if camping in a place they don't intend to come back to. If you are down on your luck in Arkansas, you don't give a toss about whether your 1974 Buick is spoiling the view of the woods. Life here is a struggle.

Are we expecting the correctional facility to be a fun kind of place? I don't think so, and it isn't. As if to rub in the fact that nobody here is going anywhere, a tiny crop-spraying aircraft is ducking and weaving around the perimeter fence, literally a few feet from the ground. Nothing else moves, not even the head of the guardroom attendant who has to call inside the razor wire for an escort for me and the camera team, an imposition that she seems to regard severe enough in itself to merit prison time.

I am in Arkansas to test a thesis: one wing of this prison has been, in effect, privatised and handed over to religious zealots. They have been allowed to choose roughly a hundred prisoners, all volunteers for the wing, and make them good. They will do so by banning television and introducing Jesus. Many Americans, understandably, are worried; should there be a trade-off between promising to be a Christian and getting better treatment in jail? What about Jews or Muslims or atheists? What about imposters?

I call it a wing. It is actually one large room, that reminds me of my boarding school. Dozens of small beds are lined up just as they were at school, but way too close together for comfort among kids, let alone big adults with tattoos and body-building pasts. The men, all dressed in white vests and

148

trousers, are in various states of repose, some lying on the beds staring into space, some sitting up reading, some in little huddles talking. Around the room piles of possessions are neatly tucked underneath each bed. At one end you can see the showers and the open lavatories, but the place still has that stale smell you get when too many human beings live for a long time in too small a space. And some of them are here for a very long time. Some are murderers, drug dealers, armed robbers. As I enter this room and smell the smell and take in the sight of it all, I am ready to believe two things: that the Christians are up to no good and that the prisoners are here for the beer as it were, for the prospect of better treatment and quicker release. Neither, it turns out, is true. Again American evangelism does not conform to the bigoted stereotype of the British press; I have not stumbled upon a plot to brainwash vulnerable souls. I have stumbled upon a bunch of highly committed Christians doing their best to help people the rest of society does not want to think about and making what appear to be incredible strides. They are receiving love, many of them for the first time ever.

The man who runs the programme is a humorous black Arkansan called Scott McClean. His interest is in tackling recidivism, not capturing souls. We watch a session on "authentic manhood" where a group of prisoners, twenty perhaps, watch a video of a pastor talking about how men can lead, in marriage and in life, without having to be violent or boorish. The Bible, we hear, makes it plain that men are the leaders (love, honour, and obey!), but they have to earn respect, not demand it. Laugh if you want to. I must say I felt like giggling more than once and these ruses and strategies are not to be tried at home – unless home is in the Deep South of the USA – but the point for me was the kindly intent. One of the principal causes of anti-Americanism is our horror at their religiosity, and yet here at the cutting edge where the evangelicals are doing their thing, they suddenly seem less hideous, less bogus, less out-of-this-world.

And an hour or so talking to the prisoners was a humbling experience: prisoners like Bobby Lyttle, four years into a seventeen-year sentence for manslaughter. Lyttle is large, a white man with a *One-Flew-Over-the-Cuckoos-Nest* stare and rheumy, sad eyes. "I took a man's life," he says flatly. "Ain't no going back on that." But he adds, in his previous life the slightest disagreement would have led to physical violence, or, as he puts it: "I would have bust you up." Now, thanks to the efforts of Scott McClean, he has changed. He has given his life to Jesus. Does Bobby Lyttle's theology – he now believes that the Bible is literally true – make sense? Would it stand up in a debate at the Oxford Union, with, say, Richard Dawkins on the other side? On both counts, no – of course not. But this man, whose life was a mess, has found a purpose. And he has found it courtesy of American religious conservatives: these folks did it.

The Innerfaith programme is highly significant. It runs in prisons in several states and there are important issues to be decided regarding its legality and future funding. Yet I have never seen a single article about it in a British newspaper. It does not fit the stereotype of the American evangelical. Their faith (the barmier the better) we know well; their works, we ignore.

Religious people are apt to talk of their lives as journeys – towards God, towards Heaven, sometimes just towards what seems to be right and good and decent. American Christianity has itself been on a journey in the Bush years – a journey to the top of the hill, to a place from which you can lord it over your fellow citizens, and a journey back down again. The journey has not ended but takes place now on lower ground. Many American Christians are happy for that to be the case, happy to get on with their work, without involvement in a political effort to supervise and organise and revolutionise the wider nation.

In 2004 I remember listening with incredulity to a radio interview with the father of a soldier who had died in Iraq. This, the father said, "was a spiritual war". The British writer Jonathan Raban heard the same interview and used the transcript in his book, *My Holy War*. The father may well have been in shock, searching for meaning in a personal catastrophe, but his words still seem almost chilling in their simple-minded, yet rather arrogant trust in George W. Bush and in, for want of a better phrase, the God of War:

> The people who don't understand just need to dig into their Bible and read about it. It's predicted, it's predestined. Benjamin understood that the President is a very devouted (sic) Christian. Ben understood

that the calling was to go because the President had the knowledge, and understood what was going on, and it's far deeper than we as people can ever really know. We don't get the information the President gets...

As Raban points out, this information of which Benjamin's father speaks is not the kind available to you and me, to post-Christian Europeans. It had been passed from God to President Bush. Many, many people believed this. Some still do. But fewer. Americans have lived through the fever that gripped them for so many years after the attacks of 9/11. At times, in the middle of the night, as fighter jets swooped outside and Dick Cheney and Bush huddled in their undisclosed locations, it seemed as if the fever was untreatable and the patient would die. There was an atmosphere of crazed, faith-fuelled fervour, often unlinked to any real threat or wise perception of what the next threat might constitute. As Raban put it in 2004, "It's as if America, since September 11, has been reconstituted as a colonial New England village, walled in behind a stockade to keep out Indians."

That was then. Long before the coming of Obama the mood had changed. And another grieving parent brought it home to me. I met Marion Gray in the cavernous indoor yard where, doused in water to keep the heat and dust down, giant cutting machines hack into marble slabs, slicing them into manageable sizes before the process of fine cutting begins: the process of turning this stone into headstone. In the town of Barry, Vermont – where, as far as I could see, there were no other industries – they cut most of the headstones for America's fallen warriors. Mrs Gray whose son Jamie was killed in Iraq, happens to be a local woman. Small, bright-eyed, occasionally tearful, often laughing, she has a fierce determination that the war should be seen ultimately as a success, but she had none of the arrogance, none of the religious bluster Jonathan Raban and I had heard in that interview in 2004. Jamie, she told me, "had died so that Iraqis could have the kind of life he had enjoyed; so that Iraqi children could live as he had lived, having fun in freedom and space". To be sure, this view is open to challenge on grounds of realism; it was also sweetly ethnocentric; Jamie had grown up on a farm on the top of a Vermont mountain surrounded by conifers and wilderness. Nobody in Iraq is going to know Vermont-style freedom, not ever. But Jamie had gone to Iraq to help. If this was a mission from God, it was a New Testament mission. In America's military affairs, the Old Testament talk is over, at least for now.

In American society and in the organs of the American state, in its politics, in its soldiery, in its self-perception, the nuttiest flavours of religious fervour have been transformed into Christian vanilla. They have not faded away – that will never happen in a nation born as America was born and sustained as it is by an overarching belief in faith and work. But for the moment, the madness has passed.

7. Guns and Violence

LORI ANN LEWIS-RIVERA Lori Ann Lewis-Rivera was killed
at two minutes to ten in the morning, close to where I live
in Washington. It was October 3rd, 2002. She was 25, married with a three-year-old daughter. She was shot once,
while standing in a petrol station, cleaning her car. At three
minutes to ten there had been birds singing, cars pulling in
and accelerating gently away, people wandering by. At two
minutes to ten came a sound "like a tyre blowing out" and
a little girl lost her mother, on a street in the well-heeled
suburbs of the capital of the free world.

When I first came to America, I had the same view of the
right to bear arms as most visiting Europeans: it seemed
crazy, to put it mildly, that a nation with pretensions to
civilisation could welcome the arming of so many people,
and the mayhem that results; the "accidental discharges",
the school shootings, the disgruntled office workers wasting
their former colleagues.

It also seemed odd that so many otherwise decent,

reasonable people would feel that the second amendment to the constitution, which the Supreme Court ruled in 2008 gives *individual* Americans the right to carry guns, might be the source of such passionate support; why not expend this energy backing other freedoms, other causes? Do guns need friends?

Then came the Washington snipers; sinister heavily armed characters, tooling around town in an old car like a duo in some Hollywood exposé of the dark underbelly of US life. Only it wasn't Hollywood. They were real – very real to those of us who lived here. They terrorised my newly adopted home city by shooting people at random over a period of three weeks in 2002, eventually killing ten and injuring three. Lori Ann Lewis-Rivera was one of the victims. The *New York Times* columnist Bob Herbert went to the scene:

> If you stay in the business of reporting long enough, you can begin to feel that you're always walking in the footsteps of violent death. As I jotted notes describing the spot where Ms. Lewis-Rivera fell, it reminded me of the notes I'd taken in August at an intersection in the Bronx where a 10-year-old girl had been shot in the head and killed by a man who, according to police, was firing wildly at somebody else. I scribbled in my notebook that the stain of the girl's dried blood on the sidewalk 'was about the size of a dinner plate – you could see where the blood had seeped into the ridges of the cement'. I never did a column on that murder, in part because it was too routine. The

kid-killed-by-stray-bullet story had already been written
so many times in so many places that there wasn't much
to add.

To a newcomer from overseas, arriving with two small
children, it all seemed very grim. I remember anguished
conversations with my wife about what the chances were of
our children being shot if we took them to the park. In
Brussels, where we lived before, the greatest threat to them
in parks was the ubiquitous dog-pooh. America seemed
crazy, out of control, deranged. As Herbert put it, "The
nation is saturated with violence. Thousands upon thousands of murders are committed each year. There are more
than 200 million guns in circulation. Murder is so routine,
including the killing of children, it doesn't even warrant serious news coverage in most cases."

The Washington snipers were eventually caught and the
suburbs are calm again; but Bob Herbert's words echo still
in the ears of all thinking people here – and particularly for
those making the case that the United States is a decent
place to live and a decent influence on the world, these are
facts which have to be faced. I make no claim that guns
added to our life, liberty or the pursuit of happiness that
autumn in Washington. Nor did they add to the freedom of
the students of Virginia Tech, on that awful day in 2007
when a mentally disturbed student, Seung-Hui Cho, killed
32 people in two separate attacks, before committing suicide.

The university is a long drive from Washington and I

arrived in the evening having set up a meeting with a group of students in the local Starbucks. We drank coffee, ate sandwiches and talked for a couple of hours, and what fascinated me was the total agreement among these students that, in the end, guns were part of life. Whether that was a good thing was less clear. The discussion included European-style horror at the fact that a man, any man not just a deranged man, could have found it so easy to buy two handguns, one semi-automatic. These were not hunting rifles, remember; as so often is the case in America's worst mass killings, you look at the type of weapon used and think afterwards, "Well, what do you expect? What else is this gun *for?*" But on the other end of the scale there was acceptance, real acceptance, even as the dusk was closing in on a place where so many young lives had just been snuffed out, that this was the price America paid for one of its freedoms. One boy wondered whether the killings might have been stopped if the university had allowed students to carry guns on campus and the victims had been given the chance to fight back. None of the students I talked to supported a British-style ban on almost all guns. It made them queasy, even in the shadow of an atrocity. In this corner of rural Virginia, guns, even that night, were forever a part of life. There was no other way.

There was some talk of new gun control measures in the wake of Virginia Tech: talk that was quickly damped down by none other than Harry Reid, the leader of the Democrats in the Senate. Even the Democrats – the home in recent decades of metropolitan angst about guns – did not see Virginia Tech as a wake-up call. In the 2008 Presidential election, neither Hillary Clinton nor Barack Obama campaigned for widespread gun control. In case they might have been tempted to try, the Governor of Montana, a fellow Democrat by the name of Brian Schweitzer, put it like this:

> In Montana, we like our guns. We like big guns. We like little guns. We like shotguns. We like pistols. Most of us own two or three guns. Gun control is hitting what you shoot at. So, I'd be a little careful about blowing smoke up our skirts.

Never mind that one of the candidates, now president, was acknowledged to be, and still is, in mortal danger from a madman with a gun. When I mentioned Barack Obama's Secret Service protection – their job, to keep him alive – in a piece for the *Ten O'Clock News,* there was a feeling among some that I had crossed a line that should have been left uncrossed. Yet the truth is that ordinary Americans were, and are, very aware of the dangers this man faces, and were aware too that they came principally from an attack with a gun. He was not at risk of being stabbed. In a black-owned hairdresser's shop in Charleston, South Carolina, the owner told me, "I think he could die. I look at his young family and I pray for him but I fear for his future, I really do." My colleague, Toby Harnden from the *Daily Telegraph,* went to Memphis for the ceremonies marking the 40th anniversary of the killing of Martin Luther King and reported:

> At the main bus station in Memphis, a city blighted by
> urban decay and split evenly between blacks and whites,
> the grim prospect of Mr Obama's assassination was
> raised several times without prompting. "People say that
> if he makes it, someone will have him killed," said
> Cheryle Boyd, 47, a cleaner. "They say it would be the
> Ku Klux Klan or maybe the Mafia, the ones that got
> John F. Kennedy. I'm trying not to let it worry me. I
> pray that if he is elected, then he serves his time and goes
> on with his life. But he's black and if he wins the presi-
> dency over a caucasian then it would be trouble. There's
> some I know that has voted for Hillary because they say
> that Obama wouldn't last a year."

Those depressing views, which no one dare call unrealistic,
are born of the gun culture and its impact on American
public life.

There are two traditional European views about why
America does not get to grips with guns. The first – the
friendlier towards the US – is that the nation is in the grip
of the evil National Rifle Association and other groups hell-
bent on mayhem; crazy guys in Montana who, through the
vicissitudes of the political system, have the ability to hold
the nation to ransom. This view essentially sees Americans
as victims of a conspiracy involving a gun-mad minority
who keep the murders ticking over and prevent peaceful
Americans from having their say. The gun lobby is certainly powerful and certainly determined; and often appears to
take a view of the right to bear arms that leaves many
Americans frustrated and depressed. This from a

Pennsylvania TV station in 2008:

> Handgun owners won't have to report lost or stolen weapons to police, after a proposal was rejected by the Pennsylvania State House of Representatives. The law would have required owners to file a report within three days after discovering a missing gun. The National Rifle Association claimed the bill could have unfairly persecuted law-abiding gun owners.

Blimey.

That news report suggests to me that there is something else afoot; this is not a story of a pressure group overcoming the good sense of a silent majority. The arguments of the NRA sometimes seem so flimsy as to be beyond comprehension. If the nation really took them on, they would be toast. But the NRA knocks on an essentially open door; America is not ready to give up guns. This attachment to guns – and more particularly this attachment to the rights surrounding guns, for instance, not to have to bother to report that a gun has been stolen – cannot be understood within the confines of our European anti-gun culture, a culture that sees guns as machines that kill people, nothing more.

Turn then to the other view the anti-Americans have of guns in the modern US: that there is something visceral about America's attachment to weaponry – something deeply ingrained in the psyche of a nation forged (that geography again) in the unique manner of the United States. America haters see gun violence as endemic in a nation whose national myth celebrates the violent conquest of the continent. They pretend that the space between the shining seas was actually teeming with friendly, native peoples at peace with each other and happy to trade with the white settlers, if only the whites had behaved themselves. Violence, and eventually guns, came from the settlers. When the settlers won, the guns won. And they have been part of US society ever since. Ziauddin Sardar and Merryl Wyn Davies make the claim in *Why Do People Hate America?*:

> In the history of America, both mythic and real, individual and communal violence created the state. Unable to provide justice and security and to be an effective instrument of law, the state continued to legitimate the recourse to individual and group violence to ensure the self-preservation of the people... The Western, the definitive American genre, is not merely a hymn to violence – it is a view of the essential, inescapable and enduring necessity of violence to preserve civilisation.

Are they on to something? You could argue that the last really successful Western was *Brokeback Mountain*. A Western produced today as a "hymn to violence" would have little success except among professors of film studies hoping to reconnect with a lost art form, but let us leave that minor point to one side.

The truth is that some of the early European invasions of South America were brutal in the extreme but were ultimately governed by the norms and the power vested in governments and the Roman Catholic Church. But in what is now the United States, although British monarchs were enthusiastic receivers of tobacco and potatoes and other wonders from the West, they did not have the power or the interest to keep on top of the enterprise. The British Crown left the settlers largely to their own devices, allowing foreigners and people of diverse religious backgrounds to settle in British territory. Until the disastrous effort by George III to tax the colonies really took off, they had been left socially and economically alone. That is probably one reason why America so quickly became independent when other parts of the western hemisphere took so long. It is true also that the lonely settlers found that there was a lot of space, most of it uncultivated, unsettled, and much of it dangerous, particularly to foreigners with no clue about survival in local conditions. As I noted earlier, it was tough. And there was, for centuries after the settlers arrived, no government in the interior to help out when negotiations were to be held or disputes to be settled.

Sardar and Wyn Davies paint the classic anti-American picture of gentle, cheery natives – always victims – being raped and pillaged by the foul Europeans. Modern scholarship – as reflected in Charles C. Mann's wonderful *1491* – suggests a more equal relationship, with the hostility felt by the settlers towards those they regarded as morally inferior beings often reciprocated by the Native Americans. But no matter; the central point is that America was born in violence. It was. That is a fact. Guns mattered. You can use this fact to bludgeon modern- day America or you can get over it; that is your choice. But to hope that America, under wiser, post-Bush leadership, might "tackle" guns, really tackle them with a view to getting rid of them in a European-style change of heart, is to hope in vain. The good people of Pennsylvania might one day have to report a lost or stolen weapon, but they will never have to hand them in.

When you show an American a gun; when you ask an American, particularly an American living outside New York or San Francisco, to handle a gun, to feel the barrel, to toy with the safety catch, to look through the site, *they will not be seeing the same thing as you.*

They will be seeing a means of self-defence, a means of imposing justice, a means of keeping decent folks safe. You (the European) will see only the killing machine. Who is right? Both, perhaps. But to try to understand American gun culture through the prism of the European view is to set yourself up for failure. Reasonable people looking to give America another chance in the years after the 2008 election should be willing to try to grasp the mentality that has led to the gun, and above all to grasp the difference between an affection for guns and an affection for violence.

The film-maker Michael Moore and others have claimed that the two are linked: that gun crime and what he sees as America's innate violence feed off each other. One of the oddest moments in his much lauded *Bowling for Columbine* – a documentary about the infamous Columbine High School massacre of 1999 – was Moore's attempt to link the violence of the killers with the fact that there was a defence industry plant making rockets nearby. In the film he asks a bemused employee, "So you don't think our kids say to themselves, 'Dad goes off to the factory every day, he builds missiles of mass destruction. What's the difference between that mass destruction and the mass destruction over at Columbine High School?'"

Well, there's quite a bit of a difference, it seems to me. American affection for guns certainly leads to death and destruction – but the idea that America's assertiveness in defending itself against Soviet attack, and in maintaining those defences in the modern world, leads children naturally into the ways of mass murder surely stretches logic too far.

Moore and other anti-Americans (you do not have to be a foreigner to make the grade) suggest that affection for guns is actually a symptom of a deeper malaise – while Canadians can possess guns but refrain from killing each other, America is, for some reason, perhaps to do with its founding, uniquely violent; that Americans are, as individuals, psychologically wedded to violence. It is a violence rooted in the evil designs of the first settlers, but responsible for widespread slaughter today. To go back to the thesis of *Why Do People Hate America?*, Sardar and Wyn Davies suggest that the whole place is like a scene from one of those old-fashioned Western movies they so enjoy, and upon which they base so much of their knowledge of the United States:

America is not only a nation in which random violence is an everyday occurrence; in which the possibility of being shot by a mugger for the sake of a few dollars or a wristwatch is a routine fear of any citizen; in which drive-by shootings and armed road rage are common… (it is) a place where mass slaughter has become a commonplace for the depressed, disaffected, and disturbed.

Oh, come off it. This goes to the heart of the jaundiced European view of the United States, the great myth of American nastiness. Yes, there is violence here. Yes, it is fuelled and sustained by a culture that accepts (embraces) guns. But there is more: there is also a tranquillity and civility that most British people can only dream of. A British man I met in Colorado told me he used to live in Kent but moved to New Jersey and will not go home because it is, as he put it, "a gentler environment for bringing the kids up". New Jersey: home of *The Sopranos*! Brits arriving here, clutching their copies of *Why Do People Hate America?* and hoping to avoid being slaughtered on day one of their shopping trip to Manhattan, are, by day two, beginning to wonder what all the fuss was about, and by day three have had the scales lifted from their eyes. I have met incredulous British tourists in New York who have been shocked to the core by the peacefulness of the place – the lack of the violent undercurrent so ubiquitous in British cities. In British market towns. In British villages. "It seems so nice here," they quaver. Well it is! And this is Manhatten. Wait till you get to London, Texas, or Glasgow, Montana, or Oxford,

Mississippi; or better still, Virgin, Utah, where every household is required by local ordinance to possess a gun. Folks will have guns in all of these places. If you break into their homes, they will probably kill you. But you never feel as unsafe as you feel in England.

I wonder what Sardar and Wyn Davies (or Michael Moore) would make of the epidemic of stabbings that dominated the headlines in the UK throughout much of 2008, or of a report in the *Guardian* newspaper in the same year on the violence visited in a gun-free English market town on Sophie Lancaster and Robert Maltby, two friends confronted by a drunken gang. When paramedics arrived at the scene, "They could not tell Lancaster's sex and both victims were covered in blood and prints from their attackers' boots. Both were in comas and Lancaster died thirteen days later without recovering consciousness".

Could it be that America is not unique in harbouring violent crime? Could it even be (take a deep breath now) that guns – legally held guns– contribute to peace?

I am with a camerawoman, knocking on the door of a very smart house in Georgetown, one of the most pleasant places to live in the entire United States. The street is cobbled, the townhouses two or three stories high, some brick-built, some clapboard. The scene is wealthy: the equivalent of Chelsea or Hampstead, on a smaller scale. The door is opened by Gillian St Lawrence, an elegant and poised woman in her late twenties. She is dressed in pearls and an expensive-looking power suit. She lets us in and offers us coffee. We chat for a moment and then agree that we should be getting on: the time has come to go up to her bedroom.

We are here to see her gun.

It is big. From under her bed she pulls it out: a Mossberg Maverick 12-gauge shotgun. She opens the case and picks it up; unselfconsciously she shows me how she could crouch down to use it, protected by the marble of her *en suite* bathroom. She is on one knee, now, pointing the gun at the door. Gillian St Lawrence is serious. "Would you kill someone?" I ask. Her reply suggests to me that this little show is not bravado – it is for real: "You can never know till it happens."

Gillian St Lawrence is a southern gal, she grew up with guns and is comfortable with them. She was showing me her shotgun as part of a campaign among residents of Washington DC to be allowed to carry handguns. Under Washington's very strict local laws, the rights to carry concealed weapons, available in most of the rest of the United States, were drastically reduced. But that changed in 2008; this was the case that went to the Supreme Court in which the Justices ruled in favour of the pro-gun campaigners. Gillian won the right to get her handgun. Then candidate Obama had nothing to say on the subject.

Is Gillian St Lawrence mad? Or bad? Or violent? She makes her case calmly, with the gun now lying on a coffee table in her sitting room: "The criminals all have guns. They can get them easily and they can get them whether or not it is illegal. I have a right – a right guaranteed to all Americans

– to defend myself." One of the statistics the Washington gun campaigners often quote is for the incidence of burglary *where a homeowner is in the home.*

The suggestion is that in the United States such an invasion, and all the dangers that go with it, is relatively rare. Only a small number of burglaries – thirteen per cent was one of the figures quoted by one of the groups (the International Law Enforcement Trainers Association) backing the gun campaigners. The figure they found for the UK was 59 per cent. Around half of attempted burglaries in the UK and other Western nations, they suggested, were conducted with a homeowner in the house.

I don't want to get bogged down in an argument about statistics, but anecdotally there is simply no question that the right to defend a home changes the dynamic when someone comes calling without permission in the middle of the night. British people know this. They might be told that gun violence in the US is appalling, and in many respects it is, but in gun-free (legal gun-free) Britain do we really feel safer? Or are we whistling in the dark?

I talk regularly to my friends in London where we used to live and where guns – let's face it – are also readily available. There the only people with guns are – by definition – the criminals. In the United States you can fight back. In the United States *the burglars are frightened of the homeowners.* The burglars are frightened of the homeowners? Is that so crazy? In our south London house the opposite is the case. All my friends in our London street have burglar alarms and bars on the windows and our neighbours' conversations are dominated by the latest break-in. I was struck by a story one told about how he'd been woken by the sound of breaking glass and looked out of his window to see a man taking things out of his car. My friend opened the window and shouted, but far from creeping off into the night in fear of buckshot in his bum, the thief seemed outraged that he was being challenged – he shouted back and carried on.

My friend tells this story as a kind of badge of honour – with respect for the *chutzpah* of this fellow. There's a name for this: the Stockholm Syndrome, a condition first identified by Swedish psychologists after hostages in a bank heist sided with their captors. My friends in London were probably rather cross the first time their car was broken into, but over the years the syndrome has taken its toll. In "violent gun-ridden America" we haven't caught it. Where we live – in a privileged but by no means wealthy suburb of Washington – we do not expect to be burgled. We do not expect our cars to be damaged. We have no bars on the windows, no alarms, and one flimsy lock on the door. We had a bicycle taken from the garage once and our neighbours' car was stolen; they had left the keys in it. Suburban America is remarkably free of the kind of petty violent crime that scars Britain. Part of the reason is that the criminals are not the only ones who are armed.

Do innocent people die as a result of America's gun culture? Yes, of course.

Shanda Smith lost two children. In 1993, her son

Rodney, home for his first holiday from college, was driving with his fourteen-year-old sister Volante through a part of Washington where people do lock their doors and bar their windows. The two were shot dead in their car: mistaken identity, said the police. Shanda Smith told me she had heard the gunfire and wrongly assumed her children were OK. "What is the point of more guns?" she asks. "It would be like the Wild West."

The argument goes on. I feel for Shanda Smith and there is a compelling logic to the notion that no guns – really, no guns, legal or illegal – equals no gun crime. And that means a deranged man in a university or a school can kill fewer innocent people before being overcome. And yet the *Why Do People Hate America?* notion that the whole nation is cowering behind domestic fortifications, or popping out to the shops with a 50-50 chance of getting mown down, is simply nonsense. The moderately wealthy suburbs of America and the small towns, where most people live, are more peaceful than their British equivalents. Guns might or might not have a role in contributing to that peace, but the peace is real.

8. Politics

The former president of Tanzania Julius Nyerere once asked, "Why haven't we all got a vote in the US election? Surely everyone with a TV set has earned that right, just for enduring the merciless bombardment every four years." Having reported four presidential election campaigns, from the Kennedys to Nixon, Carter to Reagan, with their Zeppelins of platitudes, robotic followers and rictal wives, I can sympathise. But what difference would the vote make? Of the presidential candidates I have interviewed, only George C. Wallace, governor of Alabama, spoke the truth. "There's not a dime's worth of difference between the Democrats and Republicans," he said. And he was shot. What struck me, living and working in the United States, was that presidential campaigns were a parody, entertaining and often grotesque. They are a ritual danse macabre of flags, balloons and bullshit, designed to camouflage a venal system based on money, power, human division and a culture of permanent war."

John Pilger, January 24th, 2008

SUICIDE IS A serious subject and mass suicide even more so – but we had to laugh, those of us sitting on the press bus

171

inhaling fumes from a dodgy exhaust system, at the start of another day on the road with Barack Obama.

"Oh God," someone called out, "they'll think we did it on purpose if we all die here; they'll think we drank the Kool Aid." You will remember that "drinking the Kool Aid" is associated with followers of the American cult leader Jim Jones, who were persuaded by him to commit suicide. They drank bottles of pop (actually Flavor Aid not Kool Aid but Kool Aid has stuck) laced with cyanide. A total of 913 people died. To this day nobody knows why they did it. How apt that the first of my 2008 journeys with the Obama team began with a Kool Aid reminder.

Obamamania was a real phenomenon. But McCain too had a history as a darling of the press; although fewer female journalists wanted to sleep with him (according to my un-scientific survey on the subject), nonetheless in the run-up to the 2008 election, plenty of reporters imbibed greedily the McCain legend of rugged non-partisan independence. So what did the battle come down to? Will history look back on the election of 2008 as a serious contest of ideas and visions, or a Kool Aid-fuelled junket with voters' final deci-sions determined by manufactured images devoid of real meaning and substance, and journalistic impressions based on subjective judgements? In other words, what were we covering, those of us who racked up the big miles in 2008? Was it a circus or a seminar, did this process owe more to Billy Smart or Thomas Jefferson?

The circus is never far from town. And sniffing the

elephant dung is important. It tells you who has the biggest elephants and how they are performing. It can give you a heads-up. An example from 2008: the defining battle on the Democrats' side was of course between Hillary Clinton and Barack Obama. The battle went on and on and on, and much smart money was spent on the notion that Hillary would eventually either squash the plucky challenger, or he would implode and she would be the default winner. I never bought this idea – I should admit openly here that I wrote her off far too early but that is another story – preferring instead to rely on the fact, and it is a fact, that American political campaigns need magic to survive. This is not a process built solidly on rational behaviour.

So it fascinated me that on the Hillary Clinton plane the magic had plainly been lost. Efforts to take some shots of the interior met with broadly based hostility: No, the Clinton people said. We don't like having our photo taken – and here's the bit that caught my attention: "The other reporters don't like to be on camera!" Hunched in their seats, protecting their privacy and writing their acid prose, these folks were not having fun.

On the Obama plane, on the other hand, the atmosphere could not have been more different. Drinks were served early and often. There were tense moments, of course, but generally the sound of laughter echoed up and down the cabin. At the front, you could spot Barack himself kneeling on a seat grinning from ear to ear.

He kept his cool, even at the height of the long war with

the Clintons. Somewhere over Ohio, my enterprising BBC cameraman caught sight of Obama up in the comfy seats and took some shots. He saw this and wagged a finger jokily, before ambling down to chat. For a man under intense scrutiny, a man soaking up the pressure of the entire Clinton war machine, he was supremely relaxed. The BBC, he said, had better be careful: "You don't want me to investigate you back there," he told me. "That's the wild end of the flight."

Once he was back in his seat and we were taking off, there was an effort to roll an orange from the back of the plane to the front. The BBC attempt was hopeless, but a producer from Fox News scored a bullseye, and the candidate's languid arm plucked the orange from the aisle. There was applause and a sense of connection between us and him. And yet of course there was none. Part of the genius of the Obama campaign was its discipline and the protection of its candidate from any unhelpful exposure. This orange-rolling nonsense, Obama's easy affability, all of it was in a sense a front, a manufactured mood, just as the Clinton dourness probably masked some jollity behind the scenes. But it felt important at the time and I said so at the time.

So is John Pilger's point made: that the whole thing is a nonsense, a sham? I don't think so. 2008 was full of bullshit but to stop at the bullshit, to go no further, is to misunderstand America's political core.

I am in a corridor in a high school in the place where, every four years, the presidential jamboree begins. The school is in Polk County on the outskirts of Iowa's dinky but rather wonderful capital city Des Moines. I say the outskirts, though so far as I can see Des Moines is all outskirts – the city centre has one skyscraper, a solid sensible structure much wider at the bottom than the top, but apart from that there are very few buildings which go above two or three stories – there is no need. There is space here. This is the flat, rich, farming country of American legend. Painted barns, rolling fields, emptiness. The nearest big city is Chicago and that's five hours with your foot down.

The date is March 2006, and I have come to see local Republicans gathering to organise local elections but also – almost accidentally – to influence the choice of their party's 2008 presidential candidate. As with most similar gatherings around the world the real keenies have a slightly crazy air – I hear one berating another for "taking liberal positions" – but before I have a moment to consider what those positions could be, a pimply youth approaches me. He's wearing a leather flight jacket and chinos and he has one of those security man's wiggly wire contraptions coming out of one ear. "Sir, did you record that conversation?" he asks. "No," I lie. And off he goes. Oh boy, we are in amateur land here. Serious security of the kind you get from the Secret Service when you really are important, is (as I claim elsewhere) an American art form. The agents are groomed, polite and utterly menacing. A Secret Service agent – if he really thought I was doing something wrong – would have ripped the tape out of my recorder with his teeth and swallowed it before handing it back and insisting that I had a nice day. A serious agent would also have known, of course, that openly recording a conversation in a public place is perfectly legal, even in these challenging times.

But I am not complaining: far from it. I was in Des Moines in a moment of calm before the storm – a brief interlude of accessibility that disappeared in a haze of press buses and photo ops by the time election year came around. The woman I was talking to – and recording, so that I could remember afterwards what she said – was at the start of an effort to become one of the most recognisable women in the world: America's First Lady. Ann Romney, a statuesque blonde, was telling me how her father emigrated to America from a village near Maesteg in south Wales. He came here looking for a better life and his daughter has unquestionably found it. She's the wife of Mitt Romney, the former Republican Governor of Massachusetts, who was the runner-up in the effort to become the Republican choice.

I remember trying to get close to him during the campaign; he simply blanked me as a useless foreigner. But on this day in 2006, this hugely successful multimillionaire businessman turned politician – tanned skin, suspiciously dark hair, very sharp suit – arrived unannounced in a modest saloon car, spent some time being polite to the Republican ladies selling coffee for 25 cents a cup (that's roughly fifteen pence) and then slipped into the back of the school theatre and pretended to be fascinated by a discussion of whether the Polk County Republicans' candidate for the school board could, under standing orders, be adopted without formal card vote. In the end proceedings were inter-rupted and Mr Romney was called to the podium, where he talked of his wife ("the boss", ha ha), his five children and his support for local politicians in their fights with the Democrats. He did not – of course – mention the presiden-cy. That would have been a ghastly blunder – akin to jump-ing into bed before even flirting, which in Iowa is something only farm animals do. The audience stood and clapped and at the end many shook his hand – it was all very warm and gentle and wholesome, a fitting way to begin the selection of a presidential candidate in a nation which, for all its com-plexity and sophistication, has a simple homestead gentility at its core. Months before the campaign teams had been fully assembled, months before the halls had been booked and the image consultants consulted, and the balloon man-ufacturers checked out, this was ground zero of the American presidential process.

After his speech, Mr Romney sat and ate a sandwich with me and the two local reporters who had bothered to attend the event. The only slight hiccup was when he tried to pay for the coffee: Romneys do not tend to carry small change and the Ladies did not take $100 bills, so there was a little bit of a fuss gathering the necessary pieces before all was set-tled.

Fast forward to 2008, to a town very close to the last scene. Dick and Ethel Schellenberg are expecting company. Their little house on the prairie glistens, dusted with snow and frosted by last night's ice storm. It is well below freezing but the sun is high in the sky and the town of Corning, Iowa looks resplendent, tingling, freshly decorated by Mother Nature, sitting prettily, and waiting for the Big Day. In the distance a train hooter echoes across the empty spaces, but all else in Corning is quiet.

This Big Day is uniquely American; American in its homespun, folksy barminess; American in its unfairness; American in its seriousness of purpose, and American in its sheer imperviousness to the logic of the European way.

We Europeans think we share America's democratic process. We tend all of us to make the mistake of assuming that we *will* recognise ourselves and our mores in American democracy if we look hard enough.

But the Iowa caucuses are not of our culture, not hewn from the wood of European democracy. They have an ancestry dating back to the time of the Native American tribes who eeked out an existence here, unseen by the outside world.

Inside the Schellenbergs' winter wonderland home, there are stolid wooden knick-knacks and greeny-grey armchairs, a sensible coffee table, a couple of heavy sideboards, and a view into a garden dominated by a large-gauge model railway, the wagons glazed by the ice, frozen by the season. Dick and I stand in the middle of the room and he points out where people will sit. Mary and Tim are coming, and the Champneys and Alison Telford (her husband is a Republican so he is banned!) and one or two others, all of them friends and neighbours. And why are they coming? To begin the process of electing the most powerful man or woman in the world. In the Schellenbergs' sitting room they and their fellow local members of the Democratic Party will gather at seven in the evening. Anyone coming late will be excluded. Anyone out of town will be excluded. Anyone in hospital or incapacitated will be excluded. Anyone too shy to make a public political statement in front of his or her neighbours will be excluded. But those who make it through the snow will divide cheerfully into small groups depending on their choice of candidate. There will follow a frenzied effort by these *über*-normal small-town folk to engage in a veritably Athenian orgy of democracy.

Say Mary and Tim are sitting with Alison in the Edwards group. The Champneys are for Obama, though, and so is Dick Schellenberg: they will try to persuade Alison, Mary and Tim to give up their man and move (physically move, in this tiny room!) to the Obama section by the kitchen. I am making the details of this up because I wasn't there – I had to go to the big city, Des Moines, to report the overall result – but you get the picture; there is drama here and high politics mixed with the lower sort – marriage politics, for instance. In the end, some minor candidates are declared non-viable and their supporters invited to join others. The final votes are counted, the percentages phoned through to Des Moines, and out into the night the merry Democrats of Corning go, their duties done for another four years. I asked Dick if there were ever fallings-out at these events, which lasted beyond the evening and coloured future non-political life. "No," he said. "I think it brings us closer." And I could see what he meant. Talking frankly about politics, one grass-root talking directly to another, strengthens those roots, strengthens the whole turf. That is the genius of the caucus system.

In television, we focus on the razzamatazz of the American party conventions, on the slick TV advertising and the prinked and media-trained candidates. We focus on who is having a good time on the campaign plane. But American politics – meretricious as it can be – has a soul. And the soul is in Iowa and New Hampshire and, certainly in 2008, in all 50 states when the process of selecting the candidates who will run for office begins. My encounter with Mitt Romney in Iowa came a full year before I met the Schellenbergs, a full year before votes were cast. It feels crazy. On paper it is profoundly unserious to ask serious politicians to focus their attentions for so long on the Schellenbergs and their neighbours. And many Americans, before 2008, had deep reservations about the primary and caucus system. Many would like to see the caucuses swept away and primaries organised more fairly. But in a tumultuous year, the system delivered. Obama and McCain were created by Iowa and New Hampshire where both scored early victories. The move back to the centre ground – the central feature of the 2008 election – was born in the Iowa and New Hampshire snow.

Presidential primaries and caucuses represent the genius

of finding a way of keeping a huge complex nation rooted in small lives and small towns. Iowa is 97 per cent white, we complain. It has no big cities, we observe. Its inhabitants are farmers, not city slickers. It is too cold for door-to-door campaigning, etc etc. And yet it works, imperfectly, and frustratingly for locals and out-of-towners alike; it really does work. They scratched their chins, these rubes, and chose (on the Democratic side) a black fellow with big ears and no executive experience. And the choices counted. In Texas, the Democrats have a primary *and* a caucus. Nobody knows why. Nobody understands how it works. The result in 2008 was so opaque and long-drawn-out that by the time the final caucus tallies were made, even doctoral students had lost interest. But I stood next to a queue, on a warm evening in the early summer of 2008, and watched entire families waiting patiently for the chance to take part in this process. No such scene is imaginable in the UK.

I am in the gift shop of an art gallery in Des Moines. An art gallery? Yes, an art gallery: Iowa is a farming state but this is not the hard-scrabble life of depression-era American farmers. Iowa is not a poor state; farmland has more than doubled in value in recent years, Iowan corn is being turned into the oil alternative ethanol as fast as it can be coaxed out of the ground, and although Des Moines is not quite Dubai, it has a wealthy feel; there are galleries and cappuccino bars and fancy restaurants. Anyway, in this art gallery shop, the staff have left the phone on loudspeaker and a call comes in: "Hiya," a voice says, "it's Michelle here, Barack Obama's wife – I'm just calling to say..." Click. An assistant reaches out her arm while serving a customer, and with a practised, almost laconic deftness, ends the call. The caucuses are magical but they are also tiresome.

Every four years, Iowans lose their innocence and lose it big time. A professor at a university in Des Moines tells me a friend of his (I wonder if it was him?) came home late one night, when the campaigns had only just begun, and had Barack himself on the answer machine saying something like, "Hi, it's Barack Obama here – I got your number from a friend, and, well, I just wondered if there was any chance you might be able to help me out with this running-for-president thingy..." The "friend" was thrilled, and spent days dreaming about the size of his White House office once the campaign was over and his part in it had been properly recognised – until the ghastly truth dawned: that Barack had left the same message for 200,000 other Iowans who drove a hybrid car, or owned a bicycle, or ate out twice a week or whatever it was that attracted them to the Obama camp. By the time the caucus happened, the "robo-calls" had become universally resented as an unreasonable intrusion; hence the swift dispatch of the call from Mrs Obama in the art gallery gift shop. The point is that Iowa is not about mass politics, it is a celebration of the one-to-one relationship between an individual American and his or her putative commander-in-chief.

Iowans have dozens, literally dozens, of opportunities each week to meet all the candidates and often to talk to them. They are in diners, in hotel lobbies, in churches, in schools, in hospitals; Iowa in campaign season is like a single British rural parliamentary constituency – think Ross, Skye and Lochaber – with every single A-list politician spending all their time there. The result is dizzying. A great American political story has two voters chatting about their choices in one of the early voting states – New Hampshire actually – and one asks the other if he likes a particular candidate. "Oh I don't know," comes the reply, "I've only met him twice!"

Occasionally there are moves to dethrone Iowa or reduce its importance; why should our presidential election be so heavily influenced, other Americans sometimes ask, by a hundred thousand or so people who actually turn up to the Iowa caucuses? The answer is always the same – the connection between the mighty and the lowly. However grand a presidential candidate is, he or she has to come to Iowa and cut the mustard. They have to talk about the intricacies of their Iraq policy with farmers. These high achievers have to pause to hear about the health worries of depressed single mums waiting tables in dusty diners on the long, straight, empty roads of the Midwest – they have to talk face to face with the kinds of people you used to see in Edward Hopper paintings, people whose highest achievement is just getting by. Hillary Clinton made a classic error early on in the race. She went to a diner and talked to the waitress (so far so good), but when she left, her tip was given by her staff to the manager who failed to hand it over later as promised. Bad mistake – you could do that in New York but in Des Moines you hand the money to the server – you look them in the eye. The waitress complained and Hillary took a tumble.

So how did she recover? Well, she lost in Iowa remember, took a night flight straight to New Hampshire, and, as she put it, "found her voice". She found it by losing it, temporarily, in another diner when asked how she coped with the pressures of campaigning. Her voice trembled. Her eyes welled up with tears. "It's not a game," she reminded people. Hillary Clinton is one of the most famous women on the face of the globe and one of the most privileged. In the British parliamentary system, she would have been voted in by overwhelming margins in any of the major parties. Her efforts to be party leader would have been unstoppable. And no one outside the party would ever have had a say in the choice. The selection of leaders, even prime ministers, is private party business; in America, it is public. And even the consummate insider – a senator and wife of a former president – can comes unstuck at the hands of a rank outsider. It is not true that anyone can become president but as an outsider you have a better chance than you do in the UK of becoming prime minister.

It is true that 2008 was an oddly open and dramatic year in American politics: 2004 (the Bush re-election year) was not half so much fun. But 2008 still illustrates a truth about American public life that enemies of the nation simply cannot or will not grasp. It is the truth of real competition, and real chances for individuals to make a difference, to meet the candidates, and to do far more than simply wave balloons and go home.

And these fights, within the parties and between them, have real consequences as well. This *danse macabre* is in reality a hard knuckle fight for power that matters hugely to America and the world. American democracy has results.

George Wallace, by the way, certainly believed what he said about the two parties being indistinguishable. But the southern renegade was a racist and making the point that on that subject he felt excluded from the national party structures. This was how *Time* magazine put it in an article published in October 1968:

> An end to the dominance of the two parties is, of course, his goal. A good part of his stock speech is an attack on the Democratic and Republican parties – with both given equal time and tirade. At some point, Wallace always notes that "both national parties have looked down their noses and called us rednecks – and I'm sick and tired of it." At another point, he declares that "both national parties ought to be for law and order. They took it away from you by kowtowing to anarchists." He adds: "There's not a dime's worth of difference between either of them."

To John Pilger, this is somehow evidence of the closed nature of the US party system. Neither party had room for an outright racist in 1968? Shame on them!

The suggestion that America has no real choices in its political system just does not wash. In fact, both the

Democratic and Republican parties are cauldrons seething with a stew of ideas and competing interests. "Broad church" does not describe the half of it: these are micro-societies teeming with all forms of human life from the venal and self-serving to the most idealistic and altruistic. America's political parties are like the nation – you have to dig in to get the real flavour. Plenty stinks but plenty does not.

The recent history of the Republican Party is a perfect example of the sheer vigour of American politics. I will not bore you with how things got to where they were at the beginning of the century, but suffice to say that two things were true of the Republicans: first, they were dominated by Christians with social agendas, and secondly, they appeared set to be *the* governing party for decades – their mores and the mores of the nation seemed to be cosy together, not identical but snug.

In fact, in the early days of the Bush presidency, some on the left were openly concerned that America stood at the doors of religious rule. When Christopher Hitchens and others pointed out that the war on terror – properly characterised – was a war *for* secular values and against religious nutters of all stripes, many Americans simply did not grasp the logic. Even in the 2008 presidential race, the maverick but rather successful Republican presidential hopeful Mike Huckabee suggested that the constitution should be altered to reflect the teachings of the Bible, in other words that America should throw in the secular towel and become a fully fledged theocracy. Should religious views – on homo-sexuality, on the place of women, on how the world was cre-ated – be sanctioned and promoted by the state? Most Americans would be horrified at the idea if it were put to them in those terms, but some Christians inside the Republican Party thought they had the chance to make it happen.

The Bush years were heady times when theocracy seemed around the corner.

But it all went wrong. And it did not go wrong by chance. Partly for reasons dealt with in my chapter on reli-gion (in particular the Terri Schiavo case), but partly as well because the Republican Party itself disliked being hijacked – even by God – it seized back control of its future. Republicans like Dick Armey – the rambunctious former congressional leader – led a fight-back. Armey thought the leaders of the religious right were bullies and thugs but he also thought they put off the electorate. He pointed out to party members that picking fights with scientific facts was a dull-witted way for a political party to behave, and that the nation at large was getting sick of it. And he turned out to be right. The backlash was fierce. In the town of Dover, Pennsylvania, Republicans on the local school board had managed to get warmed-up creationism infiltrated into biology classes – and here's what happened: all eight mem-bers of the board who were up for re-election lost their seats. "If there is a disaster in your area," the tele-evangelist Pat Robertson told the people of Dover, "don't turn to God –

you just rejected Him from your city."

Mr Robertson was once an important man – the former Attorney General John Ashcroft teaches at his university; his views have been sought on Supreme Court candidates and issues of foreign affairs, and he once even ran for the Republican presidential nomination. But should those views govern the Republican Party? Many members thought not – a view that gained traction after President Bush got himself into such dire trouble during his second term. The President famously told an interviewer that when deciding to go to war in Iraq he listened to the authority not of his dad but of a Higher Father. "Look where that got him," was the reaction of many Republicans.

The consequence was the failure of a single properly paid-up member of the religious right to get onto the Republican presidential line-up in 2007. It was not just that they missed out on getting their man elected as the candidate: they didn't even manage to get a dog into the initial fight. Ever heard of Sam Brownback? No, nor have most Americans. He was as close as you could come to the authentic voice of traditional religious conservatism in this last election, but Brownback (actually a Roman Catholic) simply never took off – he was out of the race before the primaries even started. Why? Because the *zeitgeist* was against him. The party had moved on. People were polite about him but were concerned now with other matters – with Iraq in the latter part of 2007, but subsequently with the economy and the housing meltdown. The Republican Party still had balloons falling from the rafters but the concerns inside the heads of those upon whom the balloons rained down had changed and *that mattered!*

So a presidential campaign that had been all but abandoned – the private jet gone and many staff members jettisoned alongside it – was eventually reborn and John McCain became the Republican candidate. Just as he was beginning to pick up momentum, and the Christian right was beginning to panic at the prospect, I attended a rally of his in Ann Arbor, Michigan. He chose as his central theme Man-Made Global Warming – a bit like choosing Sexual Positions for Gay People at a conference of Islamic clerics. He offended almost everyone that day but cared little; I asked him afterwards whether he might not have chosen a better subject: "There are worse things than losing elections," was his characteristic reply. But he knew better, of course, he knew that he was not losing this election. He knew that the Republican Party of 2008 had been blown to the four winds. There was not a block of party members with the power to impose any orthodoxy on any candidate. Some religious folk went with Mike Huckabee but plenty more thought he was a dangerous left-winger (as Governor of Arkansas, he had raised taxes and did not approve of Wall Street salaries) and opted instead for the smooth but almost preternaturally untrustworthy figure of my old pal from Iowa in 2006, Mitt Romney. Other "national security" conservatives longed for the firm smack of Rudy Giuliani (the former Mayor of New York), while economic right-wingers toyed with (and gave millions of dollars to) the whacky Texan Congressman Ron Paul, who promised to abolish public education and end the Iraq war. It was a mess. No choice? Nonsense. All about the balloons? Bullshit.

But here is the catch in all of this that can wrong-foot the foreign onlookers, even those of goodwill; this was not about manifestos either. It was not about the policies. It was about character, and when you think of the kinds of decisions a president has to make and the distance between his or her selection in the primaries and actually getting to do anything (normally around a year), that seems to me to make perfect sense. Yes, the candidates' views on current events matter, but not as much as their likely views on likely and unlikely future events.

My education in this matter came in Michigan after that McCain rally. Michigan snow is disappointingly unplayful – it's too fine for snowballs (I suppose because of the cold) and when the wind blows horizontally (as it seems to all the time), crystals of this jagged stuff go right up your trousers. I was standing in an Ann Arbor doorway trying to stay warm with a man who worked in a nearby hotel – he had voted in the Michigan primary for John McCain. If McCain was famous for any one policy at the time of his election, it was the Iraq troop surge – he backed it publicly and loudly in 2007 and at the time was generally written off for his pains. So what did my fellow doorway shelterer make of Iraq? He opposed it, and wanted the troops out now! We had no time for a detailed debrief on the clash between his views and those of the candidate he had just trudged through the snow to vote for, but back in Washington, troubled by the encounter, I searched out the detailed exit polling data for Michigan.

Sure enough, there was a category of Republicans who said they opposed the war – and, in Michigan, most of them voted for McCain. The only candidate to have enthusiastically backed the troop surge and talked of staying in Iraq for a hundred years picked up most of the votes of those who thought Iraq had been a disaster. This feels like a mistake. And yet on reflection perhaps it isn't. John McCain was a maverick – he was unbound by ties to George Bush or to his party. He was a man willing to consider Plan B if Plan B seemed sensible. He was intellectually flexible – he would probably not have fought the Iraq War and certainly not fought it in the way it was fought – and anti-war Republicans seemed to understand this, appreciate it, and trust this man who supported a war, to bring it to an end if that turned out to be the right thing to do. Although he says he would keep US troops in Iraq for a hundred years if necessary, what people hear is "I would get them out in good order as soon as possible." They still chanted inane things at his rallies ("the Mac is Back"), and his wife Cindy was indeed a touch rictal. But there is substance here as well – McCain sold Republicans the essence of himself and it worked.

The choice was saluted thus by commentator Jonathan Rauch in the National Journal in February 2008:

Wise Republicans know, to begin with, that the party is lost if it cannot rebuild its own center and appeal to the country's. Bush-era Republicanism was all about suppressing the center and mobilizing the extremes, on the (correct) assumption that conservatives outnumber liberals. It worked, for a while, because of 9/11 and because the Democrats unwittingly cooperated . Forced to choose between the Republican Right and the Democratic Left, independents leaned Republican or just stayed home.

Unfortunately for Republicans, the Democrats wised up and started choosing candidates with centrist appeal. Forced to govern from the center of their party, instead of the center of the country, Republicans meanwhile swung too far to the right. Independents cut loose. Blood rushed back into the political center. Republicans found themselves marginalized by their own polarizing strategy. The wiser among them now understand that the only way back is through the middle.

John McCain didn't have the courage of his convictions.

The final proof I would cite of the inescapable logic of the Republican move back to the centre-ground was the disastrous choice of Sarah Palin as the McCain running mate. Mrs Palin was a hopeless candidate in many ways but principally because the things she believed in – the things that got the party faithful going – were not the drivers of this election. Americans were looking for competence and calm – with Palin they were treated to a kind of dizzy passion that led majorities to tell pollsters, again and again, that she was not qualified for the job. True, many of the faithful were delighted by her presence on the ticket. I remember a woman at a rally in Ohio telling me that she could never vote for Obama because he was "a baby killer". The woman was enthused by Palin. But the nation was not similarly enthused by the anti-abortion cause this time round. The passion of the true believers was countered by the thoughtfulness of the wider public.

Yes, American politics is also ludicrously expensive. But the wealthiest candidate (again a round of applause for my friend the multimillionaire Mitt Romney, who spent millions of dollars of his own money on the race) was beaten. And on the Democratic side, the candidate with the biggest pot (it was of course Mrs Clinton, for all her populist stuff about saving America for the little people) lost to the candidate whose personal pot was small but whose capacity to attract donors was huge. So the right to stand in 2008 could not be bought by a candidate simply turning up and slapping his or her money down. You need money in American politics but it has to be, at least in part, money you work for.

The same is true of the general election. McCain and Obama both had money-raising opportunities but Obama, through his appeal and his internet savvy, raised much more. He was awash with cash towards the end of the race, so much so that the Republicans were complaining that the election was being bought. But it wasn't being bought, it was being paid for. The appeal came first, then the cash. If Obama had been a dud, he would have raised nothing.

This last presidential campaign seemed, at times, to be unbearably long. It was flawed in many ways. But it began in places where real people live. Where real concerns were aired to real candidates. And where the voters whittled the candidates down to the two front runners with seriousness of purpose and heartfelt concern for the future of the nation. After a period of deep polarisation, the people settled down to choose between two candidates with broad cross-party appeal. There is a lot wrong with American democracy, but it is capable of reflecting swings of opinion and mood in a huge nation, and above all it has its heart in the right place, a place where coffee is 25 cents a cup and a man who would run the world must sip that coffee, wait his turn, and in the end, lose! A place where "inevitable" candidates can be tripped up. A place where ideas can catch fire. A place where character matters. A place where an unqualified Alaskan can be humiliated. There is Kool Aid, of course. And balloons. But there is substance as well.

9. Flying with the White House

WHEN BARACK OBAMA first met the chief pilot for Air Force One he did nothing to hide the fact that he was seized with childish apprehension: "You are straight out of central casting," the president said, "which is exactly how I want the pilot of this plane to be…" Nothing separates a man from the rest of humanity more than the ability to take off in Air Force One. Even coming along for the ride changes your life…

It was eight o'clock in the morning and something was very wrong. I awoke dog-tired: jet-lagged and confused. I was in a hotel in central London, travelling with the President. *Travelling with the President.* Well, I had not spent the night with him, I had not actually seen him, I did not know where he was, but George Bush and I were due on the same plane for a journey from London to, of all places, Teeside Airport, the jumping-off point for a visit to Tony Blair's home. The problem was that the plane – this iconic flying symbol of America's might – was scheduled to leave in an hour. I was in a hotel on Oxford Street. It could take an hour to battle past the Japanese tourists and check out. In other words, two missed alarm calls and a last-minute change to the President's schedule had caused me to miss Air Force One.

Or so I thought. But I failed to understand the majesty of the experience of travelling with the President; an American majesty true admirers of the US should admit openly is part of the appeal of the place: the fact that when Americans set their minds to doing something practical, there is nothing on earth that can stop them. It is a self-confidence, to be sure, which leads them into difficulties, and led them into Iraq. But in all manner of more achievable areas it does get things done. It will work for Barack as it worked for all the others since the jet age arrived.

On this disastrous morning, I career down to the lobby and into the section of the hotel the White House staff, like the generals in a conquering army, have commandeered. The signs on the doors are very temporary, whacked out on a portable printer, but very serious-looking all the same; press secretary, bag handlers, briefing room etc. The advance staff spend their entire lives setting up this paraphernalia, sometimes for a stay that lasts literally a couple of hours. But on this morning, the press buses carrying the other journalists had long gone and the staff were packing up.

I remembered a previous trip on Air Force One, a short hop during an election campaign that took us from

Andrews Air Force Base in Washington to North Carolina, just half an hour south. The press bus had got separated from the main motorcade and had tried a nifty shortcut to get back to the airport. But we hit trouble. A local policeman, to be precise, a state trooper who said, "My instructions are that nobody passes." So what happened? Did we negotiate? Did we call for help? Did we heck. The state trooper was torn limb from limb and eaten by a twenty-something-year-old White House staffer before our very eyes. With blood still dripping from her teeth, she hopped back on the bus and said one word to the driver – "Drive."

Do I exaggerate? Not much. This mighty machine waits for no man save one. Among the best ever episodes of the series *The West Wing* was the visit by President Bartlett to rural Indiana where, owing to strange time differences in different counties, the most senior White House staff were late for the return trip. The plane left and they were stranded. True to life. When the President is on board and seated, the crew do not say, "Ladies and gentlemen, welcome aboard from the flight deck – we are just waiting for a few passengers and we'll be off as soon as air traffic control give us the all clear." Uh uh. When the President is on board and strapped in, the doors close, the plane taxis – and takes off.

So it was with little real hope of assistance that I explained my predicament to the White House team clearing away their effects in the lobby of that Oxford Street hotel.

But what I hadn't grasped is that while Air Force One waits for no man, while the American side of this bargain is inflexible, nowhere was it written that other normally accepted givens – London traffic, for instance – could not be altered by an act of American will.

So they sprang into action. Curt messages into phones; no pleases, no thank yous, no goodbyes. Then to me: get in that car. And thus began the best trip to Heathrow Airport that man has ever endured. A Secret Service chap had been given the job of getting me onto the plane and he was going to do it; we drove at a perfectly relaxed but insistent pace, using the grass verges occasionally and side roads often, to the edge of the airport, where my man – who had plainly memorised the map of southern England as part of his tactical training for this mission – turned suddenly towards the planes. I thought he might be able to get me through boarding procedures quickly but I did not expect him to be able to do this: we were behind a runway on a slip road plainly used only by VIPs and police. At the barrier, we were delayed seconds – a flash of the badge and the words, "I need to get this guy on the President's plane." The policeman looked at me and I could read his mind: for a failed breakfast television presenter you're plainly doing rather well. And that was it – a cursory look at my luggage and the car drove me under the wheels of Air Force One – just as Mr Bush got aboard. I saw him and I thought *this is travelling with the president.* I was covered in sweat and bab-bling thanks but the Secret Service man was looking at his nails with the air of a chap who could manage far greater challenges.

America is able to project power on a scale that is truly imperial. As I argue elsewhere, America does not possess an empire and Americans would not know what to do with one. But the imperial reach of the US is undeniable. On that visit to Britain, when we got to Teeside Airport we were transported on to Tony Blair's constituency by Black Hawk helicopter – two of them had been flown in for that twenty-minute task. The helicopters and their pilots and technicians. Even the fuel – the fuel! – had been brought from America, lest anyone might try to tamper with the local stuff or in case the local stuff was not up to the job. None of this will change for President Obama.

Save perhaps this: one of the problems of the Bush age was that the President confused the majesty of the presidency with the majesty of the President. They are two separate things. There were those in the Bush team – Dick Cheney was their leader – who saw congressional oversight, committees asking questions and calling for White House witnesses, as a threat to the dignity of the office, and to the ability of the boss to be able to project his power. But the system is designed for the majesty to attach to the office, not the man (or woman). When poor old Richard Nixon introduced a troupe of trumpeters to the White House and had them tootle prettily when visitors came, the nation laughed and was embarrassed. This was royal-style trash: cool on a tourist trip to some teeny European country but not properly majestic. American majesty is based not on royal-style falderals, the meaningless pomp of minor blue-bloods, but on the much more impressive foundation of an ability to get things done. It is that ability that causes presidential candidates to become presidential material.

There was a wonderful film, *Journeys with George* – made by Alexandra Pelosi, the daughter of the senior Democratic Party politician Nancy Pelosi. She got access to the Bush campaign in 2000 and developed a kind of flirty, needling relationship with the man who was then a candidate – just one of the candidates – for the Republican leadership

She sat next to him on the plane. She asked him cheeky questions on the tarmac. She stood next to him on a bus. And gradually as the film goes on, as the candidate begins to become the winner, the access dries up. He isn't on the bus any more. He walks separately on the tarmac. The plane is big and there's a curtained-off area at the front. The story of Air Force One – the majesty of the enterprise – is also the story of how America's top person becomes quickly separated from the rest of us. This is not without its psychological costs. Even British prime ministers have to go home to their constituencies. They have to cajole their cabinet colleagues. They have to face John Humphrys. American presidents are free to stew in the myth of their invincibility, in the myth that the majesty has accrued to them personally. Will Obama avoid this? It's a psychological issue this, not a political one: Reagan avoided it, Clinton (as evidenced by his behaviour on the campaign trail in 2008) did not.

It's a problem for all those who come in contact with the White House. White House coverage, White House privilege, White House access, White House mystique, White House unwritten rules: all of it started with President Theodore Roosevelt. He was the first big-time politician to rationalise the handing-out of news – and help create the myth of the office. In those days – and for decades afterwards – the White House or those hoping to be in the White House campaigned the length and breadth of America by train.

Historians tell us it was tough work. America's first White House press corps would consist of 30 or 40 reporters with pencils, notebooks and strong constitutions. Candidates would speak from the back of the train, perched on specially constructed platforms. Once the speech was over, the train whistle would blast and the reporters would clamber back into the fetid press carriage whose aroma was, according to one contemporary account "a compound of cigar smoke, whiskey and the stench of men who had not bathed for five or six days". The Pullman staff would burn incense in the dining car to try to make it better.

Access was good. According to Timothy Crouse in his classic study of the 1972 campaign, *The Boys on The Bus*, the old-timers had wonderful opportunities for contact with the candidates. Joe Short of the *Baltimore Sun* lost $400 playing poker with Harry Truman during one long afternoon on the campaign trail.

People could be bought as well; the Secret Service meal

allowance was low and the chaps could be treated to a steak in return for titbits of information. Not wildly corrupt given modern-day Washington, but quite effective.

Crouse says a scholarly study of these men revealed that half had no college degree; eight had no high-school diploma and two had not attended high school at all. The report concluded, sniffily: "Men without a frame of reference and with an uncontrolled, impressionistic (rather than analytic) approach to issues are driven to a surface interpretation of events."

By the late sixties, it was all getting much more professional – the journalists better educated and the politicians more savvy. But that impressionistic versus analytic problem persisted and persists to this day. The problem is "the bubble".

Crouse writes of the boys on the McGovern plane in 1972 (McGovern was the Democratic candidate who began much favoured but ended up losing badly to President Nixon):

> The fact that [some reporters] thought that McGovern had a chance to win showed the folly of trying to call an election from 30,000 feet in the air... The reporters attached to George McGovern had a very limited usefulness as political observers, by and large, for what they knew best was not the American electorate but the tiny community of the press plane, a totally abnormal world that combined the incestuousness of a New England hamlet with the giddiness of a mid-ocean gala and the

physical rigors of the Long March.

He makes the point that because a campaign reporter's career is linked to the fortunes of his candidate, they do not "like to dwell on signs that their winner [is] losing, any more than a soup manufacturer likes to admit that there is botulism in the vichyssoise".

Now the White House is the ultimate winners' bus. When you take off in Air Force One, you see all heads on the ground turned towards you. As a reporter, you are gratified by the fact, and it is a fact, that everyone is interested in the news you produce.

The consequences are horrible to behold. One radio correspondent I know – he works for a major network and followed President Bush everywhere – was so full of himself that he found it visibly painful to converse with occasional White House press corps travellers, let alone with anyone – anyone – outside the bubble. In all the times I travelled with him, listening to his booming voice as he filed his pieces – travelling with the President – I never heard him say a single enlightening or interesting thing. That was not his job, even if he had been capable of it. As Crouse put it all those years ago: "Some reporters thrived in this suffocating palace atmosphere. They began to think of themselves as part of the White House, and they proudly identified themselves as being 'from the White House press' instead of mentioning the paper they worked for. They forgot that they were hand-

out artists and convinced themselves that they were somehow associates of a man who was shaping epochal events...
The faces of these men [in old photos on the pressroom
wall] were infused with a funny expression, a pathetic aura
of pride, a sense that they were taking part in the colossal
moments of history. Now most of those moments were forgotten, and no one remembered a word."

I suspect the Obama era will spawn a whole new generation of sycophants: "I was with Barack when he..." etc etc.
But it's not just the press who go a bit peculiar. Entire
nations have a tendency to go weak at the knees when the
White House calls. I remember a zoom through Germany
with President Bush – a visit that was to be over in a matter
of hours. In a rather eerie fashion, the German authorities
cleared all civilians off the streets. The effect was utterly
deadening – totalitarian. It was like a film awaiting the
arrival of the extras. The President and the Chancellor conducted their business quite happily but there was, I wrote at
the time, a lack of genuine warmth because there was a lack
of genuine people to be seen. The German authorities had
an unpopular US President dropping in and their reaction
was to suppress their own people with a vehemence utterly
out of keeping with any sense of proportion or democratic
decorum. It was an attack of the vapours, caused by the
arrival of Air Force One.

Our next stop on that trip was a place where democracy
was a slightly more recent fashion, and one that had not
entirely caught on. In Bratislava, the capital of Slovakia, to

their credit they did at least allow protests to take place but nowhere near the President. Outside the White House hotel riot police were everywhere. I got up early and went to a cavernous press centre to talk to the *Today Programme*. Big mistake. My way back to the hotel was blocked by the police who appeared to believe that I was on a mission to attack the President, a belief that could not be shaken by any number of accreditation cards. They demanded a passport and I explained that I didn't have it – the White House deals with all that.

The situation was becoming slightly out of hand when I spotted a Secret Service agent leaving the hotel. Now as you know, I am an admirer of these men and women, but the problem did truly feel insurmountable.

But boy, did he pass with flying colours. He was not a big man but he was trim and muscular and walked with an air of easy confidence. Up to the crowd of goons he came and delivered the line, "American Secret Service – I need him in here."

The goons briefly considered clubbing us both to death, but only briefly. The Secret Service carries with it the weight of the entire armoury of the world's only superpower – each grey-suited officer is a modern equivalent of Lord Palmerston, requesting and requiring that foreigners keep their hands off you. It works with the Metropolitan Police guarding Heathrow, it works with the *Dixon of Dock Green* crowd in central Bratislava. In every civilised country it works, because in every civilised country, America counts. I don't know how much of my US taxes goes to fund the Service but it's not enough.

On that trip to Bratislava, by now successfully unarrested, I returned to the bosom of the White House and vowed never to leave. I told my friend Alex Russell of the *Financial Times* what had happened and he looked genuinely concerned, as if I had had a Near Miss. To a White House correspondent, leaving the bubble is both courageous and foolishly risky, off-piste skiing for politicos.

Of course, all of this majesty, and the reaction to it of the press, and of foreign governments, is hugely frustrating to those who would do America down. They complain – legitimately in some respects – that the way the White House travels, at home and abroad, is symptomatic of a failure to get to grips with the real world; it is a projection of power, but also of carelessness. Presidents do not explore the world; they cruise across it like elderly people on a luxury ship, calling in to the occasional port to buy knick-knacks but never penetrating the interior, and never wanting to. Even President Obama – who has travelled the world more than most of his predecessors – cannot be immune to this tendency.

Well alright. But the majesty is still capable of being pricked. Americans keep a grip on the Imperial Presidency; a tighter grip than some might realise. Ever since the time of John Adams, the nation's first vice president and second president, there has been a tension surrounding the amount of organised prestige that should be attached to the great offices of the American state. Adams made the mistake (he had spent time in France and Britain which had perhaps affected his judgement) of suggesting the new title of President of the United States of America was insufficient: His Majesty the President was one of his alternatives or at the very least His Excellency the Commander-in-Chief. It was never going to fly. People laughed as they did at Mr Nixon's trumpeters. Americans respect the office of Head of State without ever entirely getting bowled over by it.

The great BBC journalist Alistair Cooke told the story in a 1966 *Letter from America*, of one Meyer Sugarman, of Glencoe, Illinois. Mr Sugarman was getting married and had intended to spend his honeymoon at a hotel in the Catskill Mountains in Upstate New York. Unfortunately, his plans coincided with those of President Lyndon Johnson, whose staff took over the hotel. Mr Sugarman received a telegram informing him that his reservation had been cancelled to make way for the presidential party. But Mr Sugarman understood the limits of the majesty of the White House. He fired off a telegram of his own, which read: "My honeymoon reservation cancelled Friday for convenience of your party. Very disturbed. Please correct."

It worked. He had his honeymoon.

Alistair Cooke – old-fashioned stickler that he was – was rather shocked by this outcome; the transcript of his talk ends with the thought that "we have played down the duties of democracy and had a ball with its privileges". But the truth is that the privileges of American democracy were always contained in, or at least implied by, the constitutional framework in which the White House exists. The White House is awe-inspiring. The President of the United States is the most powerful person in the world. But he or she is also constrained by rules, and more importantly, by that wonderful American ability to puncture pomposity. Richard Nixon famously came to a sticky end after believing that he was above the law; but Watergate was only one of the areas in which he was brought back to earth with a bump. His trumpeters did not last long either. The White House is grand but it is American, and American grandeur is tempered by the history of a nation that was founded by grafters with little time for ceremony. The founding fathers had farms to tend. The regal progress of the White House around the world is certainly something to behold. The journalistic coverage of these trips should embarrass those who seriously claim that America knows enough about the world to be able to lead it. But America is a nation of self-righting mechanisms. Air Force One is not a symbol of oppression; it's a symbol of confidence and power, neither of which ought to be feared.

10. So What is Wrong with America?

THERE ARE VERY few occasions on which I want to strangle American friends, but the temptation becomes almost insurmountable when I hear them say: "Oh my Gosh!"

What they mean is: "Oh my God!"

But in polite American society, even this mild blasphemy is unacceptable.

So people hedge their bets, mind their language and blur the edges. The result is that life in the American suburbs is lived, linguistically at least, in soft focus "la-la land".

People warble rather than talk, and inoffensiveness is raised to the status of a major virtue. Don't get me wrong; American politeness *is* a major virtue – but American linguistic timidity is a vice. You see it especially at Christmas, which has now become "the holidays" in all but the deepest reaches of the Bible belt. Why? Out of fear of offending atheists, or Jews, or occultists, or Moslems or Hindus? It is potty. For one thing, none of the above-mentioned could possibly be offended, or if they were, they should not be;

wishing someone a happy Christmas cannot be considered an act of aggression, cultural or otherwise. But more importantly, isn't this nation all about assimilation? Isn't it all about adherence to the core values of the Anglo-Protestant settlers who landed at Plymouth Rock and kicked the whole game off? Americans might not put it as starkly as that but in a nation in which ninety-something per cent believe in God, it does seem odd to me that the word Christmas is so underused. I long to hear someone say, "For God's sake, have a happy Christmas..."

If you think too much about the offence you might cause by telling someone something, you begin to lose track of what the something might be. You begin to value everyone being happy above anyone knowing the truth. The *New York Times*, for instance (America's self-styled newspaper of record, printed an obituary for Earl Butz, a little-remembered politician from the Nixon era who had finally come unstuck campaigning for Nixon's successor:

> Mr. Ford had been counting on Mr. Butz to help win the Midwestern farm vote when he ran for a full term against Jimmy Carter in 1976, and Mr. Butz campaigned strenuously in that race. But his career in Washington suddenly ended a month before the election. On a plane trip following the Republican National Convention in August, accompanied by, among others, John W. Dean 3rd, the former White House counsel, Mr. Butz made a remark in which he described blacks as "coloreds" who wanted only three things – satisfying sex, loose shoes and a warm bathroom – desires that Mr.

Butz listed in obscene and scatological terms.

I read that piece and wondered at its coyness. The journalist and author Christopher Hitchens, implacable enemy of the inoffensive, was on hand to let rip:

> There isn't a grown-up person with a memory of 1976 who doesn't recall that Butz said that Americans of African descent required only "a tight pussy, loose shoes, and a warm place to shit." Had this witless bigotry not been reported accurately, he might have held onto his job. But any reader of the paper who was less than 50 years old could have read right past the relevant sentence without having the least idea of what the original controversy had been about. What on earth is the point of a newspaper of record that decides that the record itself may be too much for us to bear?

Hitchens went on to make a wider and more political point about the failure of American newspapers to reprint the images of Mohammed commissioned by that Danish newspaper in 2005. The cartoons were, of course, printed legally in a free society but in the months after they appeared there was, you will remember, an effort to intimidate the Western media into silence and apologies and quiescence. Americans – for all the freedom talk – were pretty near the back when it came to standing up for the Danes. Inoffensiveness morphs into cowardice in other words. Failure to speak clearly, even if offence might be caused, becomes a failure to confront issues at all, a failure in the case of the Danish cartoons to stand up for freedom against tyranny. I suspect Hitchens might be wrong about the Danish cartoons or at least guilty of simplifying a more complex issue (the problem seems to me exaggerated respect for religion, any religion, rather than over-dainty concern for causing offence), but the thrust of his case is true: the American mainstream media plays safe. Too safe.

It does so because it is largely commercially driven – who wants to offend viewers when the name of the game is gaining viewers? But there is a deeper more interesting reason for this timidity. It is cultural. Perhaps as a reaction to the roughness of the place, to the harsh Wild West saloon bar that America partly is, a suburban culture has been developed that deodorises the tangy scent of controversy from the saloon bar of everyday life. It is like keeping good cheese in the fridge. It minimises nasty smells at the expense of the richness of the experience of life. It makes you want to scream, "Enough fucking cleanliness!"

I have a friend from New Zealand living here – a normal chap and the father of three very nicely spoken children – who admitted to me that he craves indecent language so badly that he goes to the video store and takes out British films. *Sexy Beast*, set among British gangsters in the Costa del Crime, is his favourite, because some of the sentences are comprised only of swear-words. Most Americans in "la-la land" would find even the title of that film problematic. *Sexy Beast* ! "Oh my gosh!" The word sex, used in the context of fun, or in a slightly racy manner, is not normally to

be heard here. And it is not just the word. The whole world
of sexual behaviour is closed to American polite society.

Eroticism is anathema in the United States – in advertising, in art, in thought.

It is not the greatest of America's issues, I suppose, but to
European eyes American exceptionalism in this area renders
the place deeply strange. It tends to lead us to wonder about
the fundamentals of American society and of the American
way of life; it is therefore, worthy of study.

What seems to be the problem? America is the centre of
two sex industries, the pornography trade based in Los
Angeles, and the abstinence trade, based in Middle America
but with branch offices all over the nation. Both of these
trades have global reach: US porn is of course omnipresent,
but US views on abstinence and abortion have also had a
global impact on the battle against AIDS. And they are
connected here at home too: to put it crudely, sex and sin
are dangerously interlinked in the minds of too many
Americans. America is one of the least erotic places on earth
– on my television there is a choice, basically, between mainstream pap in which sex is smut, to be giggled at or air-
brushed away, and hard-core drivel in which serial couplings
are portrayed in gynaecological detail stripped of humanity
and appeal. (I am imagining this from the titles!)

There is nothing in between. A recent American radio
report about a museum of erotica that had just opened in
Oxford, England, brought it home. No one had complained! The American reporter simply couldn't believe it –

213

and was so conditioned to the words sex and complaint going together that she could not cope. She did her best to describe the museum and interview the curator but the lack of complaints was for her the biggest deal by far.

The fact is that any American reporter covering any subject with any tangential link to sex risks his or her job.

Imagine then, the upset and the outrage, the gaping open-mouthed horror, when on the programme with the biggest audience of the year – the annual Super Bowl football match – the Janet Jackson incident occurred. You may remember it, but if you are British I doubt the memory is one of your most searing. Here in the United States, it lives on. To recap the nightmare – look away if you must – 90 million people watching the half-time show saw her frock fall apart and reveal one of her breasts.

For many of the viewers it seems the experience was one of the most shocking of their lives. "Oh my gosh," they collectively intoned. Within days, there were hearings on Capitol Hill (I am not making this up) and earnest discussions on talk shows of how to save America from indecency. I saw a breakfast television presenter tell a solemn-looking weather person that her nine-year-old son had been watching. Imagine. What will she tell him? What will he think? Well, I hope he has a good memory, that young chap, because the powers that be have been coming down hard ever since on breasts and on talk of breasts.

Within days of the Janet Jackson incident, a partial view of an elderly woman's top half on a medical drama programme was hastily cut. The programme was made by the BBC and shown in full on BBC1. In America, it could not now be broadcast. The subject matter – a dirty bomb – can be discussed. They have a copy of this film in the Homeland Security office that deals with domestic nuclear threats (I know: they showed it to me) but realistic portrayal of the reaction, doctors coping with the aftermath, could not and cannot even now be shown to the wider American public. And it wasn't the bomb, stupid, it was the breast.

Of course, as relaxed Europeans would tell the Americans if only they would listen, the effort to desexualise all of public life results not only in very dull television, but in an underbelly of seediness – which is the only place left for it to go. It leads to Victorian England: chintzy gentility and child prostitution living side by side.

It also leads, in modern America, to disaster, personal and familial. I have lost count of the times, in the many years I have lived here, that an upstanding pillar of the community has been laid low by a sex scandal. And they almost never involve what one might call traditional sex between chaps and girls. In fact, quite often they don't really involve sex at all, but the whiff of it is enough. The whiff of sex and the stench of hypocrisy as human beings try to live their lives according to the bizarre and unnatural precepts of America's permanent war on eroticism.

Before 2006, most Americans would never have heard of Mark Foley. He was a minor Congressman from Florida; once thought of as a potential recruit to the Senate but quickly passed over. Nobody outside Florida or Capitol Hill had ever heard of him. Then Mr Foley, a Republican, was forced to resign after sending salacious messages to teenage male pages in the House of Representatives. The pages are essentially interns, sent by their proud parents to run messages around the corridors of Congress. Mr Foley had texted some of them his naughtiest thoughts. Ghastly indeed and several complained. Two points struck me, though. First, in spite of an FBI investigation, no charges were ever brought against Mr Foley. He broke no law. Secondly, hadn't his really odious behaviour come years earlier when he introduced a bill, the "Child Modelling Exploitation Prevention Act of 2002" to outlaw websites featuring images of children, saying that "these websites are nothing more than a fix for paedophiles". Legal experts complained that the bill would have prohibited commercial photography of children, in other words, the United States would have become the first nation on earth to ban pictures of kids out of fear that its citizens were sent into a sexual frenzy by them.

Was Mr Foley a weirdo? You bet, but paging the pages was the least of his sins.

Another case in point was the very strange business of Ted Haggard and the male prostitute. Pastor Haggard was one of those squeaky-clean-looking evangelical TV people, the ones who are (to cynical British eyes) so obviously not what they seem, that only in a nation as closed to sex as America is, could they survive. Anyway, as I mentioned in the chapter on religion, the pastor used to rail against gay

marriage, citing it as a threat to the entire institution of marriage, apple pie etc. Then, of course, he was found to have
been having a three-year-long tryst with a gay prostitute
with whom he took methamphetamine, a serious drug.
Now plainly, Mr Haggard was troubled, but would he have
had these personal issues if his ministry, his entire public
life, had not been spent so closely focused on sex? Like the
Roman Catholic Church at its worst, America has an
unhealthy obsession with sexual behaviour, and an inability
to find a niche for it in the life of the nation that allows it
to become, well, normal.

This brings us to America's continuing problem with the
rational world. I made it clear previously that I don't buy the
whole package of disdain that tends to accompany
European attitudes to American religion. The madness of
recent years is over. We should give credit to a nation that
has, to a large extent, come back to its senses. But America's
rational world problem is caused by something other than
its Christian faith, and it thrives in areas of life that are not
in the least bit religious. Halloween is the obvious example
– the Celtic festival came to the US with Irish immigrants
but took off in the New World with a vigour that suggests a
deep-seated desire to wallow in ghosts and goblins and fear
of dark forces. My children love it, of course, but every
Halloween, as we traipse around the neighbourhood picking
up sweets and admiring pumpkin heads, I feel an uneasy
sense that this festival should not be quite the big deal that
it is; something is amiss.

Many evangelical Christians agree. But who are they to talk? God in his heaven must sometimes wonder at the sheer credulousness of some of his more ardent US followers. It is, truth be told, a credulousness that renders large numbers of Americans unfit to play a major role in the intellectual life of the 21st century; unfit for any role with a speaking part and certainly unfit for leadership. American religious faith was described to me once as infantile; that is too offensive a term to be useful, I think, but the charge is interesting. I suppose I should accept my own logic and try to understand that the American religious revivals – they are episodic events – come, at least in part, as a result of the search for a better, happier world on which to focus. And it is a fact that the toughest of environments, natural and man-made, have tended to breed the most religious of souls.

We talk about the US being a religious place, and it is, but the south is where the spooky action is. The south is where church attendance really is above 50 per cent – close to 60 per cent in states like Alabama and Louisiana. Drive around the south on a Sunday morning and the chapel car parks are filled to overflowing with *Dukes of Hazard* pick-up trucks. There's a mini rush hour when the faithful all drive home, spitting chewing tobacco out of their broken side windows into the ditches bordering the endless space of the fields.

My problem though is not that all these folks go to church, it is what they are told while they are there and the way in which it translates into a crass and superstitious view of all human life. It is the effect of tin pot theology on their capacity to think straight, and by extension on America's capacity to make decent judgements – in science, of course, but in ethics as well.

An example that depressed me: a Tuesday afternoon outside the statehouse in Atlanta, Georgia. Atlanta is a modern city. It has one of the busiest airports in the world. It is home to CNN, the cable news channel that revolutionised the news business. It is where Martin Luther King preached. It has a literary pedigree as well: *Gone with the Wind* was written here. And yet on this Tuesday afternoon, the top brass of the state – led by the Governor himself (the admirably named Sonny Perdue) – had gathered not to honour human achievement or plan human improvement, but to pray for rain.

That's right. They stood on the steps of the statehouse, 250 of them, and closed their eyes and looked to the heavens. "We have not been good stewards of our land," they murmured. "We have not been good stewards of our water. Lord, have mercy on your people, have mercy on us and grant us rain. Oh God, let rain fall on this land of Georgia."

Stone Age men possessed of undeveloped brains and little knowledge of the natural world would have recognised the gathering and felt quite at home. So would many anti-modernist Moslem extremists, the characters who live in caves in Afghanistan and dream of chopping off our heads. Godforsaken simple people from throughout the sad superstitious history of humanity could have had a ball on that Atlanta Tuesday in 2007. I felt sad for a nation not fully in control of its senses. Sad as well for people so truly incapable of empathy for others who really were in dire need of God's assistance but who were not receiving it. Sad that this pathetic gathering could be so self-satisfied, so cruelly uncaring about the suffering elsewhere in the world, that they really thought God would drop his other concerns and listen to their prating on about rain. Sad that rich people in the richest nation on the face of the earth have not got the gumption to feel any of the humility that (they told me at my Quaker school) the Bible teaches.

That is the problem with the simple theologies of the south; they are destructive of educated thought and destructive of a true sense of common humanity. It is not just nonsense, it is dangerous nonsense.

Now you want to know if it did rain. It did! They chose a day with a twenty-per-cent chance and on CNN they had a weatherman report it as a kind of miracle. Shame on them.

There is a postscript to this silly little incident though and it is important because again it demonstrates that "the picture" in this complex and freedom-loving nation is never "the whole picture".

I noticed a few days later that the blogspace in the *Atlanta Journal* newspaper was filled with comments, overwhelmingly hostile to the batty Governor and his Stone-Age cohorts. Typical was this from a writer who identified himself as broker627:

SCARY!! Our government leaders are asking invisible spirits that are floating around for help with our water issue. REMINDER – HE HAS BEEN "PRAYING" FOR RAIN SINCE WE MOVED HERE IN APRIL WITH NO RESULTS SO IT'S ALL B.S.!!!" I don't believe in any of it but if I did, we should be praying for a new governor.

My favourite though was this pithy cry, so pellucid and true, from LD in Atlanta: "Good Grief, how embarrassing."

It *is* embarrassing. But I come back to the point that this is not really about religion per se but about a kind of chronic mental failure that seems to haunt the nation. Opinion polls suggest, for instance, that roughly a fifth of all Americans – really one in five – believe that the sun goes around the earth. This is more than ignorance. This is Stone Age stuff. And if you can believe that, you can – *really* – believe anything. During the height of the controversy over Barack Obama's egocentric and bombastic former pastor, the Rev. Jeremiah Wright, one of the central issues was Wright's view that HIV might have been created by the US government to get rid of ethnic minorities. It was that belief, and Wright's refusal to back down from it, that led directly to Obama's final decision to cut the preacher adrift in April 2008. But as the *New York Times* journalist Nicholas Kristof pointed out, opinion polls suggested as many as 30 per cent of black Americans thought that the charge was at least plausible. When Kristof was deluged with messages from white Americans expressing incredulity at this figure, he responded by pointing out that white America was also no stranger to conspiracy theory madness; for instance, according to a poll conducted by Ohio University, 36 per cent of all Americans asked thought US government officials might have allowed 9/11 to happen in order to bring about war in the Middle East. Kristof ended this thought with a depressing flourish: "Americans are as likely to believe in flying saucers as in evolution. Depending on how the questions are asked, roughly 30 to 40 per cent of Americans believe in each."

Incidentally, Mr Kristof is a campaigner for better education – more maths, more science – in the belief, apparently, that this might do the trick. He thinks the nation has dumbed itself down but might be capable, with some effort, of climbing out of the pit of ignorance. I have my doubts. There is something visceral about American credulousness. Something Europeans, quite rightly, find inexplicable and frightening; and just plain wrong.

But enough of this foolery. These are annoyances after all, symptoms of dysfunction but not necessarily of grotesque maladjustment. What about real, deep-down badness? What about the Achilles heel or heels? Is there a single aspect of American life of which the outside world can legitimately say, "There! You see, we knew all along you were doomed."

Just one in my view. In spite of Obama.

"This situation we've got here now – they could've solved that 40 years ago. Why didn't they? *Your* white race. Why didn't they? *Your* white race."

My white race. My British home is in south London; I am aware of race. I am aware of being white. But until that afternoon in rural Mississippi when I heard those words, spoken in a rhythmic southern drawl, I had never really sensed what it meant to be a white person in the United States, facing the anger of blacks. Clint Collier, a black man in his nineties, is still burning with rage. I am sitting with him in the tiny sitting room of his house on the wrong side of the railway tracks in fetid, steaming Philadelphia, Mississippi. Fans whirr and the wet heat is moved around the room. He is shaking: ill, I think, but angry as well. The cause of his anger is the effort by well-meaning, modern-day liberals to settle one of the most infamous crimes of segregation-era Mississippi: the murders immortalised in the film *Mississippi Burning.*

More than 40 summers ago, in the state of Mississippi, three young civil rights workers, two white and one black, were found murdered. Their deaths led to nationwide outrage in America, and did much to spur the civil rights movement. Seven men were eventually convicted of conspiracy, but none with murder. Like so many white killers and abusers of blacks in Mississippi, the murderers escaped justice because their fellow whites would never provide the evidence to convict them.

Until, that is, June 21st, 2005 when, a tad delayed, justice was visited on Edgar Ray Killen, the preacher-man who lived on the outskirts of town, and who was known by many to have assembled the mob that carried out the killings. The jury of nine whites and three blacks treated their task with care, rejected the charges of murder, but found Killen guilty of manslaughter.

Which is what brought me to Clint Collier's sitting room and face to face with the stark fact that the trial, the conviction, the sight of justice done after all these years, was but a drop in an ocean of injustice and malice and continuing bitter hatred. Mr Collier's point is that a few fancy trials (and there have been a few in recent years) do not begin to atone for the history of this state, this region, this nation.

The black–white relationship in the United States is fundamentally different to anything we Europeans experience. There is racial tension in the UK but it is focused on small-scale bigotry today, now. At its ugliest it does, of course, lead to murder – I am not trying to downplay racism outside the United States – but as often as not it is about jobs or cooking smells or house prices. And of course, in our troubled times, it is about culture as well, fear of groups of people because of the behaviour of some group members. In the United States all these prejudices and tensions and idiocies exist. But the black–white thing is different. It comes from deeper down. It comes from the whip and the cotton fields and the little children ripped from their parents and sold off like dogs to the highest bidder.

There is nothing exculpatory to be said about the legacy of American slavery. It stinks. And the stench persists. You can know this – in the sense of understanding it as a historical fact – but the enormity of the crime (I am using the word properly here: not it's size, it's ghastliness) is only really apparent after some time spent living in the United States and seeing the damage done, not just to the slaves, those nameless history-less millions who toiled and perished here such a short time ago, but to their offspring, who live here today.

Barack Obama helps. But the idea that his presidency – even if it lasts eight years – can really change the black-white balance strikes me as too optimistic, even for America. Obama proves that a black man can become president but it doesn't prove that black men and black women can lead free and equal lives, with all the opportunities the nation can offer.

From the air, Mississippi has the colour of fresh broccoli. At a distance, the trees look tightly coiled, richly green in the sunshine, with purple patches in the shade. Mississippi is home to millions of trees and not many millions of people. It is a verdant, sweaty place. As you come in to land, there are glints all around you of sunlight on still water, meandering streams, reservoirs and swamps. When blacks were killed in Mississippi, this is where, more often than not, they would end up. When the FBI drained a swamp looking for the "Mississippi Burning" victims, they found four extra bodies.

The shocking thing is that these are not facts from America's distant past. It was still happening yesterday. On a visit to Mississippi I met a wonderful man named John

Perkins. Mr Perkins, who is black, is a well-known preacher who specialises in ministering to prisoners. I met him in a young offenders' jail outside the capital, Jackson. One of his helpers at the prison is an elderly, rather frail-looking white woman named Cynthia Cockerne. The two are mighty close to the Lord; indeed I think they would say that He brought them together. The two look entirely at home in each other's company, both cheerily religious and driven by their faith. It is a relationship unthinkable until the last decade or so. As I left the prison, Mr Perkins walked out with me and announced casually, "That woman is a saint, and to think that her great-uncle killed my brother!"

The great-uncle had been a policeman who had shot the black teenager for some minor indiscretion. It was a racist killing, unpunished, indeed uninvestigated. John Perkins and Cynthia Cockerne had stumbled on their connection while chatting about their family histories. On the surface this is a rather wonderful story. Hatred and injustice has been replaced by love and reconciliation.

You can argue, I suppose, that time will heal America's racial rift. After all, the very separation of the races – the blackness of black people and the whiteness of whites – is threatened as never before by what used to be called miscegenation, interracial sex and marriage. President Obama is not black, properly speaking. He is the product of a relationship between a black man and a white woman. Not so long ago, the very idea was anathema to a large majority of Americans, certainly in the south, but those objections look increasingly quaint.

And yet the story of John and Cynthia is also a story of injustice beyond reach. It is a story of individual reconciliation that cannot blot out past hatred and its lingering aftershocks. Right now he is still black. She is still white. To see hope in the fact that a policeman in Mississippi may no longer kill black people with impunity, to see hope in the fact that a later generation has recognised the crime and is sorry about it, is to miss the wider point: that it happened very recently. Yes, it is possible for reconciliation to take place. And yes, the highest cabinet office in the land has been held by black people, Condoleezza Rice and Colin Powell. Yes, Barack Obama sprang from this land. Yes, much has changed. But this was a mighty big wrong and it went on for generations.

The fact is that the divide between white and black America worsens even as some individuals make the leap across it. A survey conducted by the respected Pew Research Center in 2007 suggested a big drop in the proportion of black people who thought their lives would improve in the future. Twenty per cent of black people were imbued with this allegedly all-American optimism, compared with 37 per cent of whites and 33 per cent of Latinos. And no wonder. Life for a majority of black Americans is relatively nasty; in every area of experience they are left behind. And the coming generations will fare no better – 70 per cent of black children are born into families with no father, no permanent man of any description, living in the household. As the black comedian Bill Cosby told me in 2007, "Little kids will grow up and they'll ask why their daddies were not there; they will blame themselves, they will lose self-respect, and so it goes on..." Cosby's particular beef is with modern American black culture which sees failure as success, depredation as classiness, ignorance as bliss. Why, he asks, should seeking education and valuing it be considered by many blacks to be "acting white"? Why indeed. Will that change under Obama? Will black people notice the fact that a black family is in the White House, and say to themselves, *change has come?* Or will this family be seen by blacks and whites as different, removed from the reality of daily life. Many white Americans, let us be absolutely blunt about it, are frightened of black Americans and would rather they went away. White flight did not end with the creation of the suburbs in the middle of the last century; it goes on today, physically sometimes, but more importantly it goes on in the minds of white people; they see a black crowd and they want to escape. And black Americans know it. Some black people reciprocate – whites in the south will tell you (privately) that black people are deliberately offensive; payback for yesteryear and for yesterday.

The two races seem incapable of normalcy. Take the Duke rape case. Duke University, in Raleigh, North Carolina, is gorgeous, set like an Oxbridge college amid generous lawns and slow, gravel-covered lanes. The day I visited, the lawns were being cut and the smell of grass was everywhere. Students, mainly white and very prosperous, were ambling between classes. It was a scene of southern splendour. But the outward calm was deceptive. Duke was in a pickle, a funk. A group of white members of the university lacrosse team had been accused of raping a black stripper they had employed to come to one of their loud spoiled-brat parties in the clapboard house they shared on the edge of the campus. Duke swooned and the nation swooned. The university did everything wrong, beginning with what looked like an attempt to hold its nose and hope the smell would pass; subsequently followed by the comprehensive rubbishing of the white boys before the case was even days old. But all caution had been thrown to the winds, all semblance of sensible, thoughtful action gone because the boys were white and the girl was black. When it emerged that one of the attackers was even alleged to have said to the victim, "Your daddy picked the cotton for my shirt", the whole nation converged on Duke like a southern lynch mob.

I talked to many white people who were genuinely distressed at the allegations; but many seemed to me to be protesting too much, to be overreacting out of a sense of collective guilt and shame. The black people in the town of Raleigh (they don't normally get to go to Duke University) were much more measured; most I talked to said they thought the attackers should be tried and if convicted go to jail, but they had no particular sense of hatred and certainly no desire for a collective punishment to assuage past wrongs.

In the event no one went to jail. The case collapsed as quickly as it had been brought, and the white prosecutor who had pursued it with such vigour was disbarred and fired. Duke had to grovel. The lacrosse players got to make speeches about sticking by each other in the face of a nation-wide rush to judgement; but this was about more than injustice; it was about an effort among white Americans to sacrifice some of their own; it was about expiation. And yet there can be none; at the end of the Duke rape drama noth-ing has changed; the history is the history and that history shapes the future in ways even the many millions of decent individuals on both sides of the racial divide seem incapable of changing.

I hope I am wrong. Many Americans, black and white, will believe I am, but many, particularly many black Americans, will agree with the words of Clint Collier, the elderly former civil rights activist in Mississippi as he dis-missed me from his living room: "Race will destroy this country, it'll bring it down, you just wait and see."

Does the progress of a man whose white mother came from Kansas and whose father came from Kenya help in all of this? The extraordinary fact of Barack Obama's rise, and of his acceptance by many white Americans as a man who could lead them, is sometimes used as evidence of real change; of the "end of the beginning" as it were, of the process of rendering race irrelevant, or at least less poison-ous, in wider American society. Colin Powell is proud of him and Powell knows about social change; he spent most of his career in the US army, which not so long ago was seg-regated. Attitudes have changed and practices have changed and the careers and lives of previous generations of black leaders have helped.

So does the fact of the 2008 election change America's racial dynamic for good? That case is unproven. It may yet be false. The slave owners committed a crime (perhaps bet-ter seen as a massive number of crimes against individuals) whose consequences live on. One historian calls race "America's Original Sin". You can deal with it, you can ask forgiveness for it, but you cannot, however hard you might try, wish it away.

Conclusion

A WISE PERSON once pointed out that although history rarely repeats itself, historians often do. Every few years, the world's brightest thinkers get together and decide that America is done for. Often Americans themselves are taken in; it happened when the Russians launched the Sputnik spacecraft in the 1950s, it happened to an extent during the Vietnam War at the time of the assassinations of Robert Kennedy and Martin Luther King, it happened again in the early 1970s when the cost of oil suddenly rose and the Jeremiahs reckoned the US economy would soon be superseded by the Europeans or the Arabs. The early 1980s saw the Japanese scare – they seemed to be able to copy anything anyone else could do and they used the money they made to buy all-American landmarks like the Rockefeller Center in New York.

Now, in the first quarter of the new century, it is happening again. The world economic crisis has shaken faith in American economic prowess. America's enemies hope that the place is finished. Even if it isn't finished, China and India are rising economic powers and there is a perception that America has lost its way; according to *Newsweek* magazine, the nation's financial woes are "largely a function of the changing economic geography and the diminished stature of the US".

That sounds bad. But it never really is. Why not? The answer to that is, of course, not clear cut and includes all manner of variables, doses of luck, and errors and missteps by potential rivals and competitors. But part of the reason why America has seen off generations of doomsayers, and is likely to do so again in this century, must be contained in the things that Americans do right.

It is true that there is great misery in America, and poverty and social and intellectual failure. There are children with no health insurance. There are religious bigots. And these things will still remain when Obama is gone. But notwithstanding America's flaws and that terrible "original sin" of slavery, this has been in many respects and for most of its history a happy nation, a functioning nation.

Go, in the summer, to the coast of South Carolina. Fly into Charleston, a city of elegance and grace but a city where a huge slave market once existed and where modern day African-Americans live mainly in dilapidated houses on the outskirts of town. Drive south (there's no public transport) on narrow country roads, where trees arch overhead and Spanish moss, which drips from the branches, sways gently in the breeze; the South Carolina low country made famous by *Forrest Gump* and *The Big Chill*. After half an hour or so, you come to a place called Kiawah Island, a place that epitomises the imperfect, but powerful message of America.

There is a gate. Kiawah is a community that welcomes strangers who can pay their way, but those who cannot are discouraged by burly men in uniforms who monitor the incoming traffic. Again that racial divide: some of the guards are black and some of the cleaners, but few of the guests. This is not utopia.

But it is beautiful and peaceful, the interior teeming with alligators and birds, and the beachfront unspoiled by humans. Kiawah is a private island – tropically hot in the summer months – devoted entirely to leisure. The canny owners have banned all the tat you normally associate with America, the gas stations and fast food joints, opting instead for tranquility. Although, this being America, the threat to tranquility from Mother Nature can never be dismissed. They have hurricanes here, and evacuation plans. But on the stormy night I have in mind, the dangers were minor: a slight chance of being struck by lightning or by an errant palm nut. Nevertheless strict precautions had been taken and one of the events planned for the evening – "Shagging on the Pier" – had been cancelled because of the storm. Shagging, by the way, is a southern dance step from the post-war years.

Disappointed, we went instead to the Ice Cream Social, which had been moved to a large shed with open sides and a sturdy pitched roof. Though soaked by the rain, no one was cold. No one, from February to November, is ever cold in Kiawah. It is a place of uniquely American warmth.

The Ice Cream Social is not the most sophisticated evening out, even for children. It begins as darkness falls. Outside, the insects and the thunder provide an exotic soundtrack but under this roof the pleasures are simple and homespun. There are trestle tables with checked tablecloths. There is ice cream. There are sprinkles. The ice cream is cheap and everyone can afford all they can eat. The children – dozens of them – sit, excited yet obedient, at the feet of a dapper, energetic entertainer, Rick Hubbard.

"Where y'all from?" asks Rick, and the adults, not the children, scream out the names of their states. Forty-year-old lawyers and teachers and accountants crying, "Maryland – Yeah!" with true feeling. It is on one level risible. (Has a British Butlins ever echoed to the sound of "Northamptonshire – Yeah!"? I doubt it.) But in the years I have lived in the US and visited Kiawah I have come to see this ritual differently.

The Kiawah Ice Cream Social is about giving vent to the attachment – a very deep attachment – that millions and millions of Americans feel towards their communities and their homes. There is nothing shameful about that. It is a part of who Americans are. And the local affection radiates out to the nation at large.

America, Rick tells the children, has never invented any musical instruments of any note, save two: the banjo and the kazoo. Whether this is strictly true, I have my doubts. But nobody in Kiawah cares. Rick plays both instruments for the delighted kids.

"Do you think we invented the French horn?" he asks.

"No!" roars the audience.

No indeed. The French horn, whatever it is, has a distant, difficult, exclusive sound to it. The banjo and the kazoo are approachable and democratic. In fact, the kazoo is so accessible that anyone can play it at any time, with no practice and no skill. It is the ultimate democratic musical instrument; all can take part.

And that is exactly how the show ends: everyone playing kazoos. Then we all drift off into the night.

There are finer beach holidays to be had elsewhere in the world. If you like the exclusivity of the smaller Maldivian Islands or the sophistication of Cannes, Kiawah is not for you. But Kiawah represents the heart of this nation – where shagging is innocent fun, and where, for your children, the Ice Cream Social is an event they will remember for ever. Sometimes, surrounded by all this holiday-camp gaiety, and mindful of those locked out of Kiawah, locked out of all the happy places in America, you can want to scream. But Kiawah fun is authentic. There is nothing hateful about it.

Obama's America is imperfect. It has no divine right to be the world's leading nation. It has no unique insight into the human condition. And yet something about it sings. Something about it works. And the election of a truly multicultural president is a a reminder that we built it: all of us, from every corner of the globe whose histories and back-grounds impacted on the minds of the people who created America and recreate it daily. It could do with improve-ment, but it is ours.

Bibliography

Bercovitch, Sacvan (1975) *The Puritan origins of the American Self,* Yale University Press

Brooks, David (2005) *On Paradise Drive: How We Live Now (and Always Have) in the Future Tense,* Simon & Schuster

Brzezinski, Zbigniew (2004) *The Choice: Global Domination or Global Leadership,* Basic Books

Crouse, Timothy with an introduction by Hunter S. Thompson (2003) *The Boys on The Bus,* Random House Trade

Evans, Harold (2004) *They Made America: From the Steam Engine to the Search Engine,* Little, Brown

Ferguson, Niall (2004) *Colossus: The Rise and Fall of the American Empire,* Penguin

Fineman, Harold (2008) *The Thirteen American Arguments: Enduring Debates That Define and Inspire Our Country,* Random House

Freedland, Jonathan (2005) *Bring Home the Revolution: The Case for a British Republic,* Fourth Estate

Greene, Graham (2007) *The Quiet American,* Vintage Classics

Huntington, Samuel P. (2004) *Who Are We? America's Great Debate,* Simon & Schuster

Leonard, John edited by (2003) *These United States: Original Essays by Leading American Writers on Their State Within the Union,* Nation Books

Mann, Charles C. (2006) *1491: The Americas before Columbus,* Granta

McClellan, Scott (2008)) *What happened: Inside the Bush White House and Washington's Culture of Deception,* Public Affairs

McElroy, John Harmon (2000) *American Beliefs: What Keeps a Big Country and a Diverse People United,* Ivan R Dee, Inc

O'Connor, Brendon (2007) *Anti-Americanism: History, Causes, Themes,* Greenwood World Publishing